Praise for *No Limits*

An inspiring and encouraging read for any entrepreneur facing the challenges of today's complex business environment. Nick Haritatos shares how he and his family left their native country of Greece to establish a new life in a foreign country, learn a new language, customs, and business practices. Nick's journey takes you through a country torn by civil unrest and war forcing him and his new wife to restart their life and growing family in yet another country. Perseverance and hard work create results in successful businesses, allowing him and his family to eventually settle in the United States where he once again proves that there are no obstacles that cannot be overcome if one puts one's mind to achieving one's goals.

Michael J. Aguilar
Brigadier General United States Marine Corps, Retired

Nick is living proof that you can create your own destiny and his story will inspire you to do the same. From his childhood in Greece to growing up and establishing his business and family in Africa to starting from scratch in the United States, Nick takes you on a journey full of both adventures and challenges. *No Limits* shows you that nothing is out of reach and I am moved by it both as a Greek immigrant and an entrepreneur myself, having opened over 50 successful restaurants. Anyone who wants to have success in business and live their dreams will love this book and the lessons in it. I highly recommend it!

John Gelastopoulos
Entrepreneur
Founder of Broken Yolk Cafe
Real estate developer

If you want to learn about success and satisfaction, and living your life to the fullest, *No Limits* is a must-read. Nick weaves a story full of inspiration, adventure and wisdom across three continents and four countries and you won't be able to put it down. This book speaks to my heart on many levels - as a fellow Greek immigrant, traveler, soccer player and long-time entrepreneur. I have a chain of successful hospitality-based businesses now but I wish I had this book available to me when I started out in business. I'm recommending this book to anyone starting a business and also to established entrepreneurs who want to take themselves to the next level. Nick embodies the book title of "No Limits" and shows you how you can too.

Takis Vartelas
President
Blue Atlantis Inc
A Hospitality Development Company

NO
LIMITS

A True Story of Challenge and Courage Across Three Continents

NICK HARITATOS

Foreword by Jack Canfield

Dedication

To Anne, my sweetie, who gladly sailed into the unknown with me many times and made my life a joy.

Table of Contents

Foreword

My mission is to help people transform their lives to maximize their potential and live their dreams. As an international bestselling author, speaker, trainer, and America's #1 success coach, I have worked with hundreds of thousands of people over the fifty plus years that I have been doing this work. And too often, I see people let fear, circumstances and what other people think limit them. They have let limits—self-imposed or imposed by others—rule their lives and stop them from achieving their big dreams and creating the life they truly want to live.

Nick Haritatos is not one of those people. He totally embodies the title of his book *No Limits*. From an early age, he has seen problems as challenges—as opportunities to find solutions rather than obstacles or barriers. That attitude, combined with his passion and curiosity, meant that, when he bought his first business at the age of 16 and became an entrepreneur, he was unstoppable. A few years later, when he met Anne, his late wife, together they were an unstoppable team. Together, they made their dreams come true. They also faced and overcame all kinds of adversity, such as starting over from scratch more than once.

Nick's life has truly been an adventure. I could not stop turning the pages of this book as I read about his life journey across 3 continents, 4 countries, 23 companies, being drafted to fight a war, raising a beautiful family, thousands of soccer games, tens of thousands of hours in the air and walking the 1200-mile California Coastal Trail.

Nick knows what it's like to be in the thick of trying circumstances. What struck me as I read this book is, no matter what life threw at him, even when the odds were heavily stacked against him, he went for it anyway. Even when others thought he was out of his mind, he went for it. Even when it seemed impossible, he went for it. Nick consistently and repeatedly defied the odds because of his trust in himself, his passion, his determination and his energy.

No Limits is the next chapter in the adventure of Nick's life, and we all get to benefit from it. Not only is *No Limits* a captivating page-turner that you won't be able to put down, but, in it, Nick also shares the wisdom he has collected and distilled from a lifetime full of adventures, challenges and successes—wisdom that is so needed in the world today. He has helped so many people throughout his life through his multiple businesses, and now he is helping many more with this book—with both the inspiration from his story plus his many "pillars of wisdom," so that you, too, can live a life full of adventure and success with no limits.

Jack Canfield
Coauthor of the *Chicken Soup for the Soul*® series
and *The Success Principles*™: *How to Get from Where You Are to Where You Want to Be*

Introduction

For the last twenty years, people have been telling me to write a book about my life. My path has been unique, taking me westward from Greece where I was born, to southern Africa, and finally to the United States. Everywhere I've landed I made a beautiful life, not because I was born into great wealth or avoided making mistakes, but because I have an unusual outlook that colors every part of my life: I don't believe in limits.

My motto is "I make events, they don't make me."

I am a maker of things, plans, adventures, and success. Throughout my long life, I've made many things, including bread, leather garments, windows, and battery chargers. I've made winning sports teams, innovative businesses, and savored a great deal of material success. I've set my feet on the beautiful earth in more than forty countries around the globe. Most importantly, I've made a beautiful marriage, a wonderful family, and life-long friends.

My life unfolded in unusual times and exotic places—influenced by war, cultural shifts, and civil unrest, as well as by unparalleled opportunities to be the architect of my own life. I've always valued my freedom to make my own choices and shaped my life around my decisions in how I invested my time and resources. This freedom of choice is more precious to me than the money in my bank accounts or any material object. I controlled my own destiny, and I challenge you to do the same.

If we were to meet in person, I'd share some of my stories. I offer you my story here, in hopes it will inspire you, regardless of your current circumstances, to make your life precisely the way you want it to be.

Additionally, for those of you who share my passion for business, you'll benefit from my business experiences and the philosophy I built over many years of business success. Golden nuggets of business wisdom are interwoven into each chapter of this book. I've also summarized them for you in the Appendix.

As you read this true story, I hope it makes you think, dream, and act on the potential in your life.

There are no limits,

Nick Haritatos

San Diego, California

November 2022

Prologue: The Baker's Boy

Every family has a story which shapes their lives. In my family, the story of what happened to my father during World War II served as a foundation and parable, providing life lessons that each member of my family interpreted differently. That story made some of us bold and others seek safety.

To understand my story, you must know my father's story first. This event occurred before I was born, but I heard it so many times, it is as if I was there.

On what had started as an ordinary day in 1940, bombs smashed into Patras, sinking ships in the harbor, and collapsing buildings. There was no warning to the destruction, no declaration of war, just smoke, devastation, and shock in the Greek coastal city. The air was full of the deafening sound of bombers, explosions, and shouting near the bakery where my father worked. Miraculously, neither the mill nor the bakery was harmed, but as the Italian bombs fell, my father's life changed dramatically.

My parents, Sofia and Panagiotis Haritatos, were born on the island of Kefalonia on the west coast of Greece. Baba's family were millers and bakers while Mama's family made their living from the sea as ship captains. When my parents became adults, they moved to Patras, the largest seaport in Western Greece. Baba, a master baker, managed the largest commercial bakery in Patras.

As the war progressed, my father and his brother, George, were called into service and sent to the Pindos Mountains in Northwestern Greece to repel the Italian forces. Baba was wounded and hospitalized. When he came home to recuperate, his recovery was cut short when he was ordered to return to the front lines while he was still in bandages.

Mama did all she could to keep the family safe as bombs continued to fall on Patras. Sometimes she had to leave the city with my older siblings and hide up in the mountains until it was safe to return home. She and some of the other mothers sheltered in caves until the bombing stopped.

The invading Italian army was not able to penetrate Greek defenses, so in 1941, Adolf Hitler sent German forces and mechanized divisions to aid the Italians and occupy Greece. The country was pivotal in Hitler's plans for world domination.

After fierce fighting, the German army broke through the Greek defenses. The battles were over, and Germany proudly occupied Greece.

My father and all the other soldiers returned home to a dangerous situation. Nazi troops controlled every aspect of life in Greece. The Nazis conscripted Baba's bakery to supply bread for their army in Patras and the surrounding cities. He was forbidden to give any of the bread to Greek people, even though many were starving.

The Nazis controlled every aspect of the bakery. My father was not allowed to buy his own flour or other baking supplies. The Nazis provided everything and told him exactly what to bake each day. They monitored how much flour and other ingredients came into the bakery and counted to make sure a corresponding number of loaves was delivered each day.

Baba was not even permitted to travel freely to go to the bakery. Every morning at 4 a.m., two armed German soldiers arrived at our home with a motorcycle and sidecar to transport my father to the bakery, then another two soldiers took him home at the end of each day.

My father had no choice but to follow orders and supply the Nazis with bread, despite how they destroyed Greece and killed so many of his fellow countrymen. He and his fifteen employees were under constant observation by armed soldiers patrolling the bakery. They feared for their lives if they failed to obey every order from the Nazis. Failure to obey would result in death by firing squad. There was also the risk of assassination by the Greek resistance for aiding the Nazis.

Baba believed in quality, even though he was feeding the enemy. He produced the best possible bread for the German troops.

Over time, he formed a relationship with the Colonel, the Nazi officer in charge of procuring bread and other food supplies. Whenever the Colonel visited the bakery for inspections with his armed guards, my father would treat him with respect. He always made something special to give to the Colonel.

In time, a mutual understanding grew between the two men. The Colonel valued my father and the delicious bread he consistently supplied and the great respect he received every time he inspected the bakery. However, the Colonel didn't know my father was engaged in a perilous mission to feed his starving neighbors.

The machines in the bakery were large and required regular lubrication. Whenever a piece of dough would touch a part of the machines, it would be stained with lubricant and look dirty. Staff would trim away the stained dough and throw it away before the loaves went into the oven. When no one was looking, Baba would wrap the discarded dough around his waist under his shirt and smuggle it home. Mama would then slice it into pieces and stealthily distribute it to our grateful neighbors.

This act of compassion was hazardous. The Nazis monitored every measure of flour that entered the bakery and observed my father closely morning and night. Somehow, my parents were able to continue this mission of mercy for a couple of years.

One night, a group of heavily armed Gestapo agents entered our house and arrested my father, locking handcuffs around his wrists and chaining his feet. They had discovered my parents' secret mission and dragged him off to jail to be scheduled for immediate execution.

At 4 a.m., when his regular motorcycle escort arrived at the house to take him to the bakery, my mother told the soldiers what had happened. Without my father, there was no one to open the bakery and produce the bread, so the soldier contacted his supervisor. Eventually, the Colonel learned there would be no bread delivery and that Baba would die before the end of the day.

The Colonel sprang into action. He called the jail commander and demanded my father's immediate release. The commander was adamant my father was a criminal who had to be executed immediately by order of the Gestapo. The Colonel gathered twelve armed soldiers and rushed to the jail. In front of my father's cell, the Colonel demanded my father's freedom. When the jailers refused, the Colonel drew his gun and ordered his soldiers to cock their weapons and point them at the jailers. Then, the Colonel shot the lock off my father's cell. The noise was deafening. Once again, he shouted at the guards to open the cell, and under gunpoint, they complied. The Colonel placed my father in the middle of his twelve guards, and they raced to their vehicles and drove away, continuing to point their guns at the jailers who attempted to follow them.

The Colonel took my father to the bakery, where he went right to work preparing the daily order of bread, surrounded by some of the Colonel's men to ensure no further interference from the Gestapo. By 3 p.m. that day, all the bread was completed and delivered as usual.

Baba never forgot how the Colonel saved his life that day seemingly just because he liked my father's bread.

I've had an unusual life, full of success, challenge, and adventure. Throughout it all, my father's story fueled and infused me with a desire for freedom, autonomy, and happiness in business and in life.

His courage made me brave. His example made me tireless. His zest for life made me strive.

Now that you know the story that shaped my life, I will share my story with you. My hope is that it will inspire you to embrace all the change, challenge, and possibility present in your experience.

Here's to a life with no limits!

Chapter 1: Growing Up Greek

The bakery smelled of warm bread and sugar. The sounds of the whirling machines and delighted customers filled me with excitement as I looked around for my father. After school, I'd run as fast as I could to reach the bakery.

"Nico, how was school today?" my father would ask as he gave me a hug.

"Fine Baba. May I stay here and watch the machines until it is time to go home?"

To a seven-year-old like me, the commercial bakery was a magical place. I loved everything about it, from the way the machines moved the dough into the ovens, the conveyor belts full of freshly baked loaves, and the busy loading bay where trucks loaded with products started their trips to stores around Patras. It was fun to watch the customers standing at the counter, looking over the display cases and selecting breads while the clerks asked them about their families. There was always something exciting to see at the bakery.

Sometimes the clerks would even hand me a sweet pastry when I said hello to them in the store.

I felt proud of my father as I watched him work. As the bakery manager, he oversaw everything. He easily lifted the heavy bags of flour and sugar and knew how to fix the gigantic machines. I liked the way he moved around the factory like an orchestra conductor, answering questions, checking the oven temperatures, and overseeing the staff.

That bakery shaped my life in surprising ways. I started to see everything going on in the bakery fit together like a giant wheel. If a machine broke or the right supplies weren't on hand, every other part of the production stopped. I noticed how carefully my father planned and organized things, so the bread was always ready at the right time for deliveries to grocery stores. He was the most important component in the bakery—getting everyone and everything to work together to get the job done.

Although I was a youngster, I absorbed the idea that business was exciting and challenging. My father was a hero. He saved our family and neighbors during the war and managed all the aspects of a complicated business operation. As a young boy, surrounded by the smell of fresh bread and the machinery noises, I decided I wanted to be in charge of a business, just like my father.

"Mama. We're home." I ran over and gave my mother a big hug around her waist.

"Oh, Nico, my darling boy, I am happy to see you." Mama kissed me all over my face before telling me to hang up my coat. I thought my mother, Sofia, was the prettiest woman in the world. She was slender with thick, shiny, black hair and her eyes crinkled up at the corners when she laughed.

Mama rarely sat still. She was always busy cleaning, cooking, or washing clothes. When she worked, she sang songs. The only time I saw her sitting quietly was when she went to Mass or said her daily prayers for us.

"Cathreen, come help me put the food on the table. Peter, Nico, go wash your hands," Mama said.

My stomach rumbled when I smelled Mama's chicken with garlic and oregano, my favorite meal. This was going to be a great night! Maybe Mama would play music after dinner, and we'd dance before she tucked me in with a prayer and a kiss.

In the morning before school, I asked, "Mama, who is Uncle George?"

"He is your father's younger brother."

"How come he never comes to visit us like the other uncles do?" I asked.

"Ah, Nico, it is a sad story," Mama replied. "Your Uncle George was very dear to your father. When you were born, he planned to name you George, in honor of his brother. However, before you were christened, Uncle George disappeared."

"Where did he go?"

"No one knows, my son. Your father has been looking for him for many years. He even hired a private detective, but no one can find George. In fact, we waited to have your baptism until you were almost three years old in hopes Uncle George would come home to be part of your special day. One night your father had a dream, and in the dream, he heard a voice tell him he should not name you George; it would be very bad luck for you. Instead, your name should be Nicolas and you were to be baptized right away. We talked to the priest and arranged for your christening, even though Uncle George would not be there.

"That is a sad story," she continued, "but there is a little part of it that will make you smile. By that time, you were already three years old. You were such a bright and happy boy and wanted to be very grown up. So, you walked all the way to the church with us, refusing to let anyone carry you. You sang and talked the entire ten blocks. Then, when the priest was baptizing you, you pulled his beard!"

When I grew a little older, Peter told me Baba worried Uncle George had been murdered.

Baba also missed his sister, who died during the civil war that followed once the Germans left Greece. He had no siblings left alive.

I noticed my father looked sad sometimes, especially in the evenings after some of his friends would come to visit. Men from the neighborhood would come to our house and talk about politics. People respected my father's intelligence and repeatedly asked his advice. I was too young to listen or understand, but they all looked serious as they talked over my mother's thick Greek coffee and pastries from the bakery.

However, most of the time, my father was happy. He had a lot of energy, like me. Baba stayed busy fixing things around the house or building things when he wasn't at the bakery. I felt grown up when he let me hold the hammer or help him. While he was fixing a window or building something, he would show Peter and me how to use the tools. He built us an ice box and even a boat.

My favorite times with my father revolved around soccer. He played soccer professionally when he was a young man. As soon as I was old enough, he taught me how to play. He'd take Peter and I out in the yard and we'd practice.

My father wanted us to love soccer as much as he did and learn how to play it properly. We'd go to watch the Patras team play every Sunday, and Baba would explain how the game worked. It was so much fun.

"Nico, Peter, come with me. I'm taking you on a special trip today," Baba said early one morning. "Put on your running shoes."

Peter and I looked at each other, then got right up and dressed as rapidly as we could. After breakfast, the three of us walked to the bus station. After traveling for a while, we disembarked and Baba said, "My sons, this is Olympia, where the ancient Olympic games were held more than two thousand years ago. Today, we are going to run around the track, just like those ancient athletes from Greece. It is important to always keep your body healthy and strong. Let's go!"

We had a wonderful time running around the dirt track. On the way home, Baba told us stories about famous athletes from Greece. I decided I wanted to be fast and strong, just like my father. I wanted to play soccer well so he would be proud of me.

I felt happy and secure within the loving arms of my family. Peter was nice to me, even though I was five years younger than he was.

Our sister, Cathreen, was eight years older than I was and always looked out for me. She was smart and particularly good at her studies. When she wasn't helping Mama or doing her homework, she would read to me, which I enjoyed.

My favorite stories were about Odysseus, the brave Greek soldier who fought in the Trojan wars and then had a journey of more than ten years to return home. I loved the way Odysseus outsmarted his enemies by finding clever solutions. There was no problem he couldn't solve. I wanted to be clever like him when I grew up.

We lived near my grandmother and other relatives, so we'd have lots of parties. Sometimes our family from Kefalonia would come to visit on their boats. Then, the parties would be very large. The house would be full of people talking, music playing, and the scents of tasty food. After a big meal, we'd all dance. Music and dancing were an important part of every happy event in Patras.

I especially looked forward to seeing my cousin Maki and his father. Uncle Angelos was a ship captain. In fact, all his brothers were ship captains, too, just like their father had been. I admired him very much. He oversaw a very large ship. He made all the decisions for his crew and had to keep them safe.

"Oh, Nico, you are getting bigger every time I see you. When are you going to come out to sea with me?" Uncle Angelos would put his big hand on my head and ruffle my hair every time he saw me, then he would laugh. I'd smile and then duck away to play soccer with Maki and Cousin Nikos in the yard.

"Sofia, something has happened. There's been a big earthquake on Kefalonia. The family will be coming. We need to get ready," my father said as he rushed into the house. We turned on the radio and heard reports that most of the buildings on the island had been destroyed, except for the monastery. I wondered how Maki and our other cousins were doing.

We all got busy. Mama and Cathreen began cooking large pots of soup. Father took Peter and I out into the yard. "My sons, people will be arriving here soon with nowhere to live until their homes can be rebuilt. We need to make space for them to sleep and stay with us for a while."

We got busy building a covered patio in our yard.

In time, people from Kefalonia began arriving in Patras. Soon twenty relatives were staying with us. Peter, Cathreen, and I gave up our beds and slept on the floor with our cousins. Mama and the other ladies cooked huge meals. Everyone talked about how thankful they were no one had been killed.

At night when things were quiet, I wondered about the earthquake. My relatives were living a regular day and then their houses fell from the shaking of the earth. I heard the breathing of my sleeping cousins nearby and felt glad they were safe. If we had an earthquake in Patras, we could go stay with our family in Kefalonia. It was good to be part of a family.

The best care came from my relatives and loved ones, and I wanted to be able to do that for them someday, too.

Chapter 2: Actions Have Consequences

"Nico don't go so fast," Mama called as she noticed me racing my bike up and down the hilly streets of the neighborhood. I was always on the move. I loved to run and ride my bike as fast as I could. When I raced with my cousin Nikos and the other neighborhood boys, I was determined to win.

My love of speed caused me several scraped knees, a broken elbow at age eight, and a terrible injury to my leg when I was ten. I had to get eighteen stiches in the back of my calf and rest in bed for a long time so it would heal. Cathreen would read me stories and spend time talking with me when I was bored.

"So, Nico, what do you want to be when you grow up?" she asked me one day. "I think you should be a dentist. They make a good living."

"Yuck, I don't want to put my hands in people's mouths all day long. I want to oversee a factory, maybe even a bakery like Baba. I like the machines and all the excitement of making things. I want to be in business and make a lot of money."

I don't know if she believed I could do it, but I know she didn't argue with me or try to push her point.

While I was stuck in my bed, I started to think about making a little car. It would be fun to ride around the hills with Nikos and the other boys in a car instead of a bike. I drew a picture of a small car with four seats and foot pedals so passengers could propel the car along with the driver. The driver's seat had a big steering wheel connected to the front suspension and the tires.

"Peter, will you help me build a car?" I asked my brother one day.

"Nico, what are you talking about?" Peter replied.

"Look at this paper. I want to build a metal car. See this picture? Would you help me? Please, Brother?"

After discussing the project with our parents, Peter and I started finding the materials we needed to build a silver car out of aluminum. As my leg healed, I resumed riding my bike and playing soccer, but Peter and I would work on the car whenever possible.

However, that car was not the only thing on our minds. Baba was unhappy and worried about the future in Greece. Since I was ten, I was old enough to be part of our family discussions. Baba read in the newspaper about how many families from Greece or other European countries were moving to countries where skilled workers were needed. Since Baba was a master baker, he believed he could make a better life for us in another country.

"Children, I've decided we need to move away from Patras. Things are rough here with the shortages of food and many men are out of work. I don't know if the government will last, or we'll have another civil war. We have no future here." Baba told us one evening. "People always need bread. We can go anywhere, and I can work. Perhaps I might even buy my own bakery. I would love to be my own boss and do things my way. I'll never have that opportunity in Patras."

Over the next year, we talked a lot about moving away from Greece. My father learned of an organization helping families move out of Europe and wrote to them for information. He would tell us each time he learned something new about a relocation.

One night Baba announced, "I've found the right place for us. It's a country in southern Africa called Rhodesia."

Peter asked, "Why Rhodesia? It sounds far away."

"Rhodesia is a wonderful country, a colony of Great Britain. It has fertile land where they grow wheat, big farms that produce lots of food, gold, and minerals. The best thing is the government is looking for men like me. They are building roads, railroads, mines, and large cities. The people love bread and eat it every day. In fact, Rhodesia is called 'The Breadbasket of Africa' because they send food all over the continent. Isn't that the perfect place for a baker like me?" Baba smiled and his eyes were shining bright. He looked happier than he'd been for a long time.

It was in that look I knew our fates were sealed and we would be leaving.

"Nico, you are a big boy now, eleven years old. I want you to help your mother and Grandmother while I'm gone. Be good and study hard." Baba rested his hand on my head as we stood in the Athens airport. I didn't want to cry, but I felt sad he was leaving. I couldn't imagine not seeing him every day.

"When will you be back, Baba?" I asked.

"I am not sure, my son. I must make a long trip to Rhodesia and then travel all around to look at everything carefully. I will come back as soon as I know if it will be a good place for us, but it may take a very long time."

All of us were sad to say goodbye. Baba told Peter he was now the head of the household and responsible for the family. Cathreen was crying a bit, until Baba teased her about boys. Soon Baba was kissing Mama once again, and then we watched him walk onto the tarmac.

Even though I was sad, my eyes couldn't stop looking at the airplanes. They were beautiful. How I wished I could fly on an airplane with my father.

As soon as Baba got to Rhodesia, he began writing us letters every two or three days. Some letters would arrive on thin, lined airmail paper. Others would be in thick white envelopes with mysterious stamps. Sometimes two letters would arrive on the same day. Those were exciting days!

Baba's letters helped us feel connected to him. I felt excited to imagine some of the things he was seeing, like elephants, jungles, and huge fields of corn, cotton, tobacco, and wheat.

He wrote that the soil in Rhodesia was red, which sounded very strange. Baba liked Rhodesia and told us stories of the people he'd met, including other people from Greece who were living there happily.

Mama would write letters to Baba every few days, too, telling him about how things were going in Patras. Peter, Cathreen, and I would write a few lines on the letters, too, so our Baba knew we loved and missed him.

I'd think about my father on the other side of the ocean and wondered what he was doing each day. I tried hard to help Mama around the house. Sometimes I'd go over to my grandmother's house to see if she needed any help fixing things, proud to use the skills Baba taught me.

Even with the added responsibilities, Peter and I would still find time to work on the silver car. After almost two years, we finished it.

On the day we took it out to the street to try it, Nikos and my other friends crowded around. They were amazed. No one had ever seen a car like it.

"Take me on a ride first, please!" Nikos cried. The other boys clamored for a turn too.

From that day on, I rode in my car whenever possible, racing down the neighborhood hills. The car went so fast, especially when I had three passengers helping me pedal.

"Hold on everyone. I can't turn the car," I yelled one day. Everyone started hollering as we began to go faster and faster. I turned the wheel as hard as I could, but nothing happened. We crashed into a fence moments later.

"Are you okay?" I asked as I got up.

"That was amazing! We went as fast as an airplane. Let's go again!" Nikos said. He and the other boys were laughing and asking me what happened. We looked at the car and I discovered the screw attaching the steering wheel to the bar controlling the wheels had fallen out. No wonder I hadn't been able to steer!

I saw a construction site nearby, so I walked over to see if there was anything to hold the steering wheel in place. I found a long rusty nail and used it to reattach the steering wheel. I wished I had some pliers to bend that nail upwards instead of letting it stick straight out of the steering column, but at least the car could steer now.

The next day after school, Nikos and two other friends, Tasos, and Tolis, came over for a car ride.

"Guys, I have an idea. Let's go over to that big hill. We'll have a fast ride," I explained.

Nikos replied, "Let's go! I bet we can go all the way down the street without having to pedal at all."

When we arrived at the base of the hill, the four of us pushed the car to the top. "Wait until I set the brake," I cautioned. "Okay climb in carefully and sit really still." As we sat at the top of the hill, my heart was racing. This was going to be the ride of our lives.

"Okay, now," I said. "If we start going too fast, I'm going to tell you to put your feet down on the pedals and slow us down. Ready? One, two, three, GO!"

We began careening down the hill. "Put your feet on the pedals now!" I cried.

Nikos was sitting by me in the front and starting yelling, "We are going too fast! Hit the brakes."

Tolis and Tasos were screaming but we kept going faster and faster. Finally, I decided we should turn into a side street to slow down, so I yanked the wheel hard to the right. The tires started screeching, the bottom of the car scraped the road for at least six feet, making a tremendous noise. Then we were airborne, flying into a ditch. Nikos went flying out of the car. Tolis bounded into Nikos's seat and Tasos landed right on top of me, shoving me into the steering wheel.

Tolis said, "Is everyone all right? Nikos, can you get up?"

Slowly everyone started to stand up. They were dirty and scraped up. "Guys, I can't move my leg." I said after Tasos crawled off me.

He said, "Nico, don't move. There's a big nail stuck in your leg." That long rusty nail I'd picked up the day before was stuck deep in my thigh, poking out of the inside of my leg.

"Oh man," Tolis said, "Look at all that blood. His leg is turning purple. We must do something."

Tasos took his two fingers and held them on either side of the nail. "Nick, I'm going to push down on your leg until you are free of the nail. It's going to hurt." Tasos pushed hard and got my leg free, then he and Nikos helped me stand up. The blood started rushing out into my shoes.

"I've got to put a bandage on this," I said, "Help me tear off the bottom of my shirt."

"How are we going to get home?" Nikos asked. "Should we carry you? Can you walk?"

"What about the car?" Tolis said.

"Let's leave it and get somebody to come and get it later." Tasos suggested.

"No, I am not going to leave my car! I can walk. Look at the front wheels, they are almost flattened. Find some rocks so we can pound them straight, then we can push the car home."

My leg was bleeding too hard for me to help, but the boys finally got them straightened out. They helped me sit behind the wheel and pushed the car slowly down the hill.

"You must promise me when we get to my house, you won't tell my mother. We'll never ride in this car again if she knows what happened. Don't tell your parents either," I said.

"Are you sure, Nico?" Nikos asked. "You're hurt pretty bad. Don't you think you should tell?"

"No, I'll be fine. Just keep this quiet, okay?"

After the guys left me and the car at home, I limped rapidly into the bathroom. Mama was in the kitchen. "My son, are you hurt?"

"It's nothing, Mama. I was running and tripped on a rock. My leg is sore but I'm fine."

The next morning, I had a terrible time walking to school. Nikos helped me as much as he could. That evening Mama asked me how my leg was feeling.

"It's fine," I lied.

After a couple of days, my leg looked terrible. It was purple and yellow. Liquid was coming out under the bandages, even after I changed them. I started to feel strange.

In school, I dropped my pencil and noticed a terrible smell from my leg when I bent over to pick it up. By the end of the school day, I was dizzy and had to lean on Nikos to get home.

"Nico, you must tell your mother. Something bad is happening to you," Nikos insisted.

When my mother heard the story and looked at my leg, she gasped. "My son, we must take you to the hospital immediately."

"Mrs. Haritatos, your son has a severe infection. I will have to give him several injections, remove the infected tissue, and stitch the wound. This infection is so advanced your son would have lost his leg if you'd not gotten him treatment today." The doctor was stern as he spoke to my mother, as if it were her fault.

I felt terrible, not just because my leg throbbed, but because this was all my doing. Mama said nothing, just looked me deeply in my eyes.

The doctor gave me some shots and then numbed my leg. When he started to cut away the infected area, the room smelled like a dead animal. After a long time, he stitched up my legs, put on layers of bandages. Some nurses took me to a room and said I had to stay overnight for observation.

Once we were alone, my mother began to cry. "Nico, you must never lie to me again or try to hide an injury. Do you realize how serious this situation was? Just imagine if I had to write your father in Rhodesia and tell him you lost your leg? I was so frightened for you."

It was terrible to see my mother cry. "I am sorry, Mama. I promise, I won't be careless again," I said as I drifted off to sleep.

When I awoke in the hospital the next morning, my mother was sleeping in a chair near my bed. After she got me home, and Peter helped her get me in bed, she said, "Nico, you are twelve years old and that's old enough to know a person might die from an infection like this. You will have to rest a long time before your leg is healed. And you are not permitted to ride your car for four months. That should be long enough for you to think about what happened."

When I was alone in my room, I started to think. I realized I made some big mistakes, first by not replacing that rusty nail and then by hiding the fact I got hurt. My biggest mistake was lying to my mother. I also thought about the danger I put my friends in when I suggested we go down that big hill. It was lucky no one else had been hurt.

I decided I had to grow up. It was my job to pay attention and protect myself and other people. I made a promise to myself I would never ignore a problem again or put other people in danger. I was going to use my head from that point on.

Chapter 3: Seeking Our Golden Valley

⟶

"Children, come quickly!" Mama cried. "We have important news from your father."

"Is he on his way home?" I asked.

Baba had been gone for almost a year. We'd all continued along in our lives as well as we could. Peter was eighteen and graduating from high school. Cathreen was twenty, and I was twelve.

I'd grown so much I wondered if Baba would recognize me. I had so much to tell him!

Mama waited until the three of us sat down, then started reading Baba's letter. He'd found a bakery to buy in Rhodesia. Our father now owned 50 percent of a commercial bakery in a city called Hartley. He wrote, "Hartley is in an area rich with farms where wheat and other foods are grown in abundance. Rhodesia produces more food than it needs and exports much of it, so it is called the Breadbasket of Africa.

"Our lives here will be wonderful! Many engineers are coming to build a highway system and factories. The country is full of growth and excitement, with opportunities everywhere for businesses. Peter and Cathreen, you are adults now and can make your own decisions, but if you decide to come to Rhodesia, I believe you will be awfully glad. You could each open a business if you wish to. There are no limits to what we can do here."

Baba's letter went on to say he would begin working in the bakery at once and prepare a home for us.

"Mama, what does this mean?" I asked.

"It means we are going on a grand adventure, Nico! We will travel to Rhodesia and join your father."

We had much to do to prepare for our journey. We decided to travel in December, after Peter's graduation at the end of the school term. We had six months to say goodbye to our lives in Patras.

Mama enrolled us in English lessons. Even though Baba wrote he'd met some nice Greek families in Hartley, most of the people there spoke English. I'd have to attend a British school and do all my homework in English, which was a little scary.

There was an organization which helped families emigrate out of Europe in those years. This organization agreed to help us on our journey, providing us with lists of required paperwork and immunizations, and helping us make our traveling plans. They also instructed us to complete health screenings and collect important documents.

It was a lot of work for Mama and Cathreen, but they were good at organizing things.

We also had to sell our house and most of our possessions. Baba wrote he'd found a house for us and would have it all ready when we arrived. We each were allowed just one small suitcase.

"Mama, what should I do about my silver car? May I bring it along?" I asked.

"Oh, Nico, I know how much you love your car. Unfortunately, it is too big to bring with us. You already realized that didn't you, my son?" Mama put her arm around my shoulders and hugged me tight. "It is hard to leave it behind. But think, Nico, you will be a teenager soon and may not fit in the car too much longer. When we get to Hartley, Baba will buy you a new bicycle, one for a young man, not a little boy."

Of all the things I had to leave behind, my silver car was the one I would miss the most. Baba wrote to say we could get new soccer equipment and other things in Rhodesia. Soccer was immensely popular in Rhodesia and Baba thought I'd easily find a team.

However, I would never be able to replace my silver car since Peter and I had made it together. I thought about my car for a long time.

The final months in Patras became a time of goodbyes. All our relatives, including our family from Kefalonia, came to visit and say farewell. There were parties and many hugs. I was twelve and too old to cry like a baby, but it was hard to imagine I'd never see my friends, cousins, and relatives again, especially my two grandmothers who were already very old. Sometimes it seemed like we were moving to the moon because Rhodesia was so far away.

However, I trusted my father implicitly. If he said I was going to be happy in Rhodesia, I believed him. I was a little sad, but primarily, I felt excited about going somewhere new.

"Nico, do you think you'll see tigers in Rhodesia?" Maki asked at one of our family farewell parties.

"Tigers live in India," Nikos laughed. "He's going to be in Africa with lions and hyenas. What do you think, Nico, will you become a big game hunter? You must promise to write us letters about your adventures."

"I'll write you both, I promise." I replied. I'd miss these cousins and my friends very much. A few days before we were to leave Patras, I took my silver car over to Nikos's house.

"Cousin, I want you to have my car." I told him.

"Are you kidding? I love this car!" Nikos replied.

"Well, you were the first of my friends to ride in this car with me, and you are my best friend. I want you to have it, on one condition: you must give it back to me if we come back to Patras."

"I promise, my cousin."

Soon the day arrived for us to say our final goodbyes to Patras. Some of our family and friends traveled with us to my grandmother's house in Athens.

That night, Grandmother's house was full of people, all supporting us on our grand adventure. I felt so excited it was impossible to sleep. I was lying on the floor of the living room, surrounded by my cousins, all of us on pallets, while the adults slept on the sofas and beds.

The house smelled of Grandmother's wonderful spanakopita and moussaka. I wondered if I'd eat those foods in Rhodesia, if I would find a soccer team, and what life would be like in such a faraway place. Most of all, I thought about how good it would be to see Baba after eighteen months.

Early the next morning, we all went to the port of Athens to a ship that would take us to Brindisi, Italy. After hugging everyone goodbye, we each took our suitcases and boarded the ship, standing at the rail to wave goodbye. I felt funny inside as we sailed away from Grandmother, Nikos, and the rest of our family. However, the ship was full of other families who were emigrating, too, so it was busy and exiting. As we sailed into the Ionian sea, I was eager to see the world. I'd never been further than Athens, now I'd be seeing Rome and Rhodesia!

When we disembarked in Brindisi, a kind travel guide met us and explained we would be escorted all the way to Rhodesia by the resettlement organization. Many more families would join our group at every stop. Our guide took us to the train station, and we were on our way to Rome.

Peter, Cathreen, and I all found kids our age within the travel group. By the time we got to Rome, we'd made new friends. I noticed Mama smiling and talking to many of the other women. Mama was very friendly and loved to meet new people. Because we were in such an exciting group, I forgot to feel sad about saying goodbye to Patras.

Rome felt overwhelming. It was such a large city.

"Mama, how many people live here?" I asked. "It seems like people and cars are everywhere." I kept turning my head from side to side on the bus so I could see as much of Rome as possible as we traveled to the airport. I wished we had more time to explore this city.

When we reached the airport in Rome, my heart started to pound. I was going to fly on an airplane for the very first time! My dream since sending Baba off was finally coming true, even if he wasn't there to experience it with me.

"Follow me, please," our guide instructed. "We will walk down this hallway to International Departures."

Everyone in our large group gripped suitcases and passports. Our family walked close together. None of us had been on an airplane and now we were going to fly for more than forty hours, all the way to southern Africa.

"Are you scared, Mama?" I asked.

"Oh, no, Nico. I am so happy to see your father I feel like I could fly without a plane!" Mama laughed.

By the time we were ready to depart, night had fallen. We walked in the freezing air onto the tarmac under the bright stars.

However, my eyes were glued to a large, shiny silver airplane. It was bigger than I ever imagined and glittering in the lights of the airport. As we got closer, I could see the four engines were already running. I smelled the exhaust and heard the loud roar of those engines. I felt like I was in Heaven to be this close to an airplane and to travel in it! My heart was pounding with excitement.

"Welcome to our flight. This evening, you are flying on one of the most modern and innovative aircraft in the world, the Lockheed Super Constellation. We have a long flight ahead of us and will make several stops to refuel the plane. I hope you have a pleasant flight." The Captain's voice boomed over the loudspeaker. We fastened our seatbelts and prepared for takeoff.

As soon as we were in the air, the plane lurched violently. People started screaming! The Captain announced we'd hit some air pockets and we'd be above them in just a few minutes. Thankfully, after that rough start, the remainder of the trip was smooth.

While we crossed the Mediterranean Sea, we slept. When we awoke the following morning, we were still flying over the water.

"Mama, can I go sit with my friends?" I asked.

"Yes, Nico, but listen to the announcements and return to me before we stop. We need to be together when we exit the plane."

I was sitting with a group of other kids when a flight attendant came by and asked if any of us wanted to visit the cockpit and meet the Captain. My hand shot into the air.

It was thrilling to meet the pilots, flight crew, and to see all the dials and instruments in the cockpit. The Captain was genuinely nice and explained all the gauges and instruments. I was fascinated and promised myself I would learn to fly a plane someday too.

Once we reached the African continent, we stopped to refuel. All of us were invited to disembark and have a meal where I had my first Coca Cola. It was so sweet and refreshing after the dry air in the plane.

After we returned to the plane, we began the long journey to Rhodesia. The plane flew low enough to see the ground clearly. When we flew over the Sahara Desert, I saw caravans of people with camels walking in the sand. The landscape changed often as we flew over mountains, lowlands with thick green vegetation, and flat grasslands. Nothing looked like Greece.

Finally, we arrived in Salisbury, Rhodesia, the capital city. As soon as we landed, I peered out of the window looking for Baba. When I exited the plane, I was shocked by the intense heat, which sucked my breath from my chest. The air looked wavy and shimmering, like water. Everything was different. There was a scent in the air I'd never smelled, the light was harsh and bright, and I could see Africans with dark skin. I wasn't sure what I expected, but in that moment, I realized I was in a new place that was utterly foreign and nothing like Greece.

I looked at Peter and grinned. He looked just as excited as I felt.

"Stay with me, children," Mama said, as we filed into the lengthy line waiting to go through Immigration. The wait seemed exceedingly long, and we all kept trying to catch a glimpse of Baba waiting for us.

Finally, after about an hour, it was our turn to approach the officer behind the big desk who spoke to us in English. Mama handled all the questions and paperwork.

Only later in my life did I fully appreciate the gravity of that experience. To me it was just one last hurdle before seeing my father. For my mother, this was a monumental moment, the culmination of eighteen months of working and planning. Our future depended on her answers and our documentation.

We all let out a huge sigh of relief when the officer said, "Welcome to Rhodesia."

We began walking very quickly toward the exit.

"I see Baba" Cathreen cried.

"Sofia, children, you are here at last," Baba said as he took us in his arms.

Mama and Cathreen were crying while Peter and I tried not to do so. Even Baba's eyes were shiny with tears as we kissed, hugged, and rejoiced in being together at last.

"Come this way," Baba said. "I have a surprise. We have a car!"

As we piled into the car, Baba explained we'd be driving seventy minutes to Hartley. While he explained about the bakery and the abundance of opportunities in Rhodesia, my eyes were glued to the windows.

Everything looked so different. The dirt was a light red color, just as Baba had explained in his letters, and the grass was a deep green. The buildings all looked very new and were placed far apart, a sharp contrast to the narrow streets of Patras with ancient buildings nestled close together. We passed vast fields of wheat, cotton, tobacco, and corn. The fields came right up to the edge of the highway. There was so much space in Rhodesia.

"Welcome home," Baba said as he parked in front of a large house.

"This can't be our house," Mama said. "It's too grand."

"Sofia, our money goes extremely far here. This is our house, and I've even hired a housekeeper to help you with the cleaning."

We walked into the house with wide eyes. It was beautiful. Baba had everything prepared. All the furniture was in place, the beds were made, and the kitchen was full of food. All we had to do was unpack our small suitcases.

We were finally in our new home!

Chapter 4: Challenges and Changes

After we rested for a day, we began to explore our new home. We had many new things to learn. People drove on the other side of the road, which seemed very strange. The cars were larger. The money was different. Most white people spoke English and came from the United Kingdom. The African people had their own languages and appeared quite different from the people in Greece.

I had never seen a person of color before that trip. I looked carefully and noticed all the ways the African people were both different and similar to me.

Several families from Greece lived in our new neighborhood. I was incredibly happy to meet Ari, a boy about my age, who showed me all around the neighborhood. We'd ride our bikes together, and I'd ask him many questions.

"Ari, I want to understand the African people. Can you teach me their language?"

"Well, Nico," Ari replied, "People here speak two languages. Their primary language is Shona. There is also another language called Fanakalo. It's a mixture of English, Shona, and a few other African languages. Few white people learn Shona, most use Fanakalo, but it is good to learn both ways to speak."

Ari and I spoke in Greek, but I asked him to teach me as much Shona as he could. I was determined to understand Rhodesia and believed that being able to speak to everyone would be wise. It was a little confusing to try to learn English, Shona, and Fanakalo all at once, but I practiced often and began to improve.

"Nico, it is time for you to begin school next week when the new term begins," Mama said one day. "We need to go to the school and complete your registration.

When we arrived at the school, I soon realized it was vastly different than my former school in Patras. When we met the headmaster, he spoke in a very thick British accent. It was hard to understand him.

"Mrs. Haritatos, we are at the start of a new school year. Based on his records, I will be placing Nicolas one year ahead of his grade in Greece," the headmaster said.

He turned to me. "Young man, you seem bright. You will need to work extremely hard to improve your English. It may be challenging at first, but this is an English-speaking school, and you must adapt. You will be the youngest student in your class. Are you willing to work diligently and catch up to your peers?"

"Yes, Sir," I replied and shook his hand as my father taught me.

The first few weeks of school were confusing. It was hard to read my textbooks in English. I'd never studied British history and now was expected to know about a long list of kings, battles, and events I'd never heard of before.

The teachers had exceedingly high expectations and offered no extra help to me except Mr. Robinson, who had just arrived in Rhodesia from Great Britain. He told me we newcomers would stick together and offered to answer questions and help me eliminate some of my confusion.

I got strange looks from the other students, as well. "Hey kid, where are you from? Why do you talk so funny?"

"I can't understand you, New Boy."

A few of the boys in my class were bullies and liked to pick on my accent. I came home from school those first weeks of the term feeling lonely and overwhelmed. I missed Nikos and my other friends. School in Patras used to be so easy for me. I had many friends and earned top marks. Now, I was struggling to understand the language, customs, and expectations in a very different environment.

My parents saw I was struggling a bit and tried to encourage me. My father said, "My son, it is not easy to move to a new country. You have much to learn, but you will do it. I know you are smart and work hard. Did you know people here are crazy about soccer? Why not find the school's soccer field and see if you can join the practices? Once the coach sees you are a skilled player, he will invite you to the team. Then, you will make friends. Soccer will always open doors for you."

Baba was right. The next day I went to the soccer field after school. I recognized a few boys from my classes and asked if I could practice with the team. Once we started to play, the boys became friendly and invited me to practice with them the next day.

After a few days, the coach called me over. "Are you new here?' he asked.

"Yes, Sir. My name is Nicolas Haritatos, and I just moved here from Greece. I love soccer and have been playing since I was a little boy. I played on city teams and for my school."

"You are a good player, Nicolas. I'd like you to join our team because we need a strong center forward. Would you like that?" the coach asked.

"Yes, Sir!"

The coach gave me the game schedule and list of the uniform and equipment I'd need. My parents were happy for me and purchased everything I needed right that very evening.

Being part of the soccer team made school much more enjoyable. My teammates liked me and started calling me 'Nick.' During the first match, I was able to score three goals and help the team win. From then on, I was accepted and well-liked by my schoolmates. Even some of the girls started to smile at me after that game.

Just like in Patras, I would visit my father at the bakery after school. The Rhodesian economy was booming, with a tremendous demand for bread. My father was busy with the bakery and worked hard. Baba and his partner had a staff of sixteen making breads and pastries for wholesale and retail trade.

In time, my siblings found opportunities as well. Cathreen opened a women's clothing business, designing, and sewing dresses. Peter went to work for an influential man from Greece, Mr. Hasson, who had a considerable number of retail stores and other businesses located throughout Rhodesia.

When I had free time, I would go exploring with Ari or some of the boys from school. Just outside Hartley, I could see water buffalos, and thousands of gazelles and other deer-like creatures. Once, I saw a leopard that was so beautiful I could barely breathe. Ari told me leopards didn't come near the road very often, so I was lucky to see one. Every night when I went to bed, I heard animals in the night.

"Mama! Guess what I saw today?" I panted as I ran in the door one day after school. "There was a huge black mamba snake on the path in front of me. I didn't see him and almost stepped right on him. I was so afraid I thought I'd wet my pants!"

"Nico, I am so glad you are safe. Your guardian angel was watching over you. Please be careful, my son." Mama hugged me tight.

Eighteen months after we arrived in Hartley, my father learned of a commercial bakery for sale in Gatooma. Gatooma was a larger city than Hartley.

"The bakery is bigger than the one here." Baba said at dinner that night. "It needs a lot of work, updating the equipment and making it more efficient. This is a fantastic opportunity for us. I could own the full bakery and not have a partner. However, we would need to move to Gatooma. What do you think?"

Peter said, "I like Gatooma. Mr. Hasson lives in that city, and I've visited it several times for my work. Gatooma has more people and better stores. I bet Mr. Hasson would have a job for me there. I vote yes."

Cathreen was eager to move to a city with more people her age. She had not found many friends in Hartley. Since she worked from our home with her clothing business, she did not see any problems re-establishing her business in a new location.

We visited Gatooma and everyone liked the city, which was much more modern than Hartley. Gatooma was in a hilly part of Rhodesia called The Golden Valley because it had many gold mines. We saw numerous large stores, factories, government offices, and even a big hospital. Gatooma had hotels, a bus system, and even a large train station.

We had many discussions around the dinner table and decided to move. My father found a buyer for his half of the bakery, and we sold our house in Hartley.

I was excited about moving to Gatooma. The school was much larger and had a good soccer team. Gatooma also had a city soccer league, so I'd be able to play at a higher level.

After eighteen months in Hartley, I understood how the school system worked and was making good grades. My English was clear, and I spoke both Shona and Fanakalo well enough to carry on a conversation. I was older and more confident than when I arrived in Hartley. Something inside me told me Gatooma would be full of golden opportunities for all of us.

After we found a new house, we moved to Gatooma and started working on updating the bakery. Peter, Cathreen, Mama, and I all worked with Baba to improve it. Baba purchased modern equipment that would increase production capacity. We cleaned everything from top to bottom and painted all the walls. Finally, we reorganized the entire facility, both the production area and the storefront, which offered retail bakery products in addition to the commercial products for stores. It was an exciting job. I enjoyed seeing the old, dirty bakery transform into a clean, modern, and efficient plant.

My first days in high school in Gatooma confirmed my belief I was in the right place. The school offered many courses and activities. The students and teachers were friendly and welcoming. On my first day, I joined soccer practice and started to connect with the other players. After a few days, I was invited to join the A team, which traveled to play against other schools. My first new friendships formed on the soccer field. Soon I had a circle of friends and felt like I belonged at the school. In Hartley, I'd initially felt like an outsider, but not in Gatooma.

Life in Rhodesia was exciting and full of the unexpected. While in Patras, I could predict my days and how I'd spend each one. Now, I was living in a land that seemed old and young at the same time. The animals, thick green vegetation, mountains, and rivers were old and untouched by civilization. Growth was all around me with new roads, railways, and businesses.

In time, I rescued a monkey I named Sally, who lived in our backyard and kept me laughing at her antics. Sally had been domesticated years earlier and was no longer able to live in the wild. She showed up in our back yard, hungry and alone, and seemed to adopt me. Every day when I returned from school, Sally would climb on my shoulder and hug me like she'd never let me go. It took a lot of work to keep her from getting into trouble as she loved to torment my mother's dog and unsuspecting visitors. When I lived in Patras, I could have never imagined having a pet monkey!

Even though I had less than two years left before I graduated from school, I was already beginning to imagine the opportunities waiting for me.

I wanted to be a business owner—that dream had never changed. I'd seen my father frustrated with his partner when he wanted to make changes in Hartley. I didn't want to report to a boss like Peter did, either. My plan was to make my own destiny and do things my way.

It was time to walk into my future and I was ready.

Chapter 5: Teenage Businessman

Within a year, our bakery was the largest in Gatooma. We had a fleet of vans which delivered in a one-hundred-mile radius of the bakery. There were two shifts of workers who produced 11,000 loaves of white bread per day, as well as brown bread and assorted pastries. After another year, it was bigger than the other three commercial bakeries combined, making daily deliveries to seventy stores in the area. In time we expanded to repurchase full ownership of the bakery in Hartley, as well as a group of meat markets, grocery, and liquor stores.

We all worked together to grow and expand. Cathreen worked in the bakery and some of our stores. My father helped Peter purchase three supermarkets outside the city near the gold mines.

One of his stores served one of the largest gold mines in Rhodesia. In that store, Peter had products for the supervisors and engineers as well as the 2,000 miners. The store was set up to cater to a wide variety of customers, with five departments: groceries, clothing, a meat market, supplies, and liquor, as well as an onsite gas station and convenience store.

The miners got paid every Thursday and the store was mobbed with customers ready to pay off their lines of credit and purchase supplies.

I usually went out to help Peter on Thursdays and had fun working the registers and talking to the customers. Sometimes my mother sat on a stool and looked out for shoplifters.

Customers would laugh and say, "Oh, Mrs. Madala, the old Missus is here, we better be good."

Our family felt like we were living in paradise. We'd left behind war and pain in Greece and built a prosperous and happy new life in Rhodesia. Because we'd been through so much, we did not let little problems worry us too much. Even a challenging day in Rhodesia was easier than things had been in Greece after the wars. We were safe, and in a place full of opportunity.

"Baba, I have an idea," I said.

Baba was accustomed to hearing me say this often at the bakery. I worked there every day, not because I had to, but because I loved it. It was fun to jump into the action and help wherever possible.

I noticed things. For example, we had eight delivery vans to load each morning. When they returned at the end of their routes, they had to be off-loaded, cleaned, and prepared for the following day. At the same time, we had delivery trucks arriving with flour, sugar, and other supplies, creating a log jam at the loading dock.

"I think we should have a schedule for the trucks. There is a lot of traffic at the loading dock. What if we changed things so all the trucks were loaded at one time and unloaded at another time instead of mixing them together?" I came up with a schedule and process to streamline loading and unloading all the trucks, saving us time and manpower.

"My son, that sounds like a wise idea. You may try it." Baba replied. He realized I had a mind for business and never disregarded my ideas or treated me like I was a kid who knew nothing. His respect for my ideas built my confidence and my love for problem solving.

The bakery had a good equipment mechanic who could fix anything. I was always curious about what he was doing and would ask him questions in Shona.

When he was in a good mood, he would teach me about how the machines worked and why breakdowns happened. Sometimes, I noticed he was busy or in a bad mood and didn't want to answer all my questions. I was probably a nuisance, pestering him for information all the time, but I wanted to learn everything possible about machines and how to repair them. My curiosity and love for learning meant I collected deep knowledge of how the bakery ran, from the product to the customers to the machinery.

I also started to go on deliveries with the drivers, bribing them to let me drive the van as soon as we were out of town. I was only fourteen and had to sit on a pillow to see over the steering wheel, but I became an excellent driver long before earning my driver's license at sixteen.

While working in the bakery and making deliveries, I began to learn more of the local languages. I was lucky language learning came easy to me, and I soon mastered Shona and Chiniaja, the two local indigenous languages, Fanakalo, and Afrikaans, one of the languages spoken in South Africa.

I noticed how surprised people would be when I spoke to them in their own language. They were always surprised and would smile at me. My parents taught me to always show great respect to everyone, and that lesson served me well.

My brain was always looking for ways to make things faster and reduce costs. My father and I were a good team. He had a passion for quality and a complete commitment to producing the absolute best bakery products using the best ingredients. With my eye for organization and cost cutting, we always found fresh ideas to discuss.

Over time, I realized time costs money, just like ingredients do. When we found ways to save time, we made more money. That idea stuck in my head, and I used it successfully all through my long career.

I also noticed I loved solving problems at the bakery. They were like puzzles to me. I liked finding ways to improve the bakery more than I enjoyed some of my homework assignments.

I also had time to watch my father work. He was very stern with the employees, never mean, but he demanded respect and compliance with the rules. Behind his back, the employees would call him 'Kamuaza' in Shona, which means 'No Nonsense.'

Baba was always teaching me lessons about how to be a man by what he said and did. "Son, you must be responsible. You are not like the other boys at school who can run around and get into escapades. You have a job here at the bakery."

He also taught me about staying healthy and avoiding alcohol and tobacco. Both of my parents were very conscious of healthy habits and instilled them in me. Some of my friends would tease me about not drinking or smoking, but I was never tempted.

When I was sixteen, Peter and I tried out for the Gatooma United Soccer Club. It was an adult club and the most popular team in Gatooma. Peter and I both earned a spot on the team.

Even though I was one of the youngest players on the team, I did my best to impress the coaches by arriving early to each practice and playing as hard as possible. I earned a place as a center forward and felt like a star. To make things even better, I scored a goal in our first home game and was amazed to receive letters and phone calls from girls who wanted to go out with me.

I changed my hairstyle to a pompadour, like Elvis Presley and Sir Cliff Richard, the famous singer from the United Kingdom. A few people started to call me Cliff, which made me smile.

Along with soccer, music was a big part of my life. I'd been taking accordion lessons since we moved to Gatooma and began learning to play the drums. I purchased a stereo system and loved to listen to a wide variety of music. My friends and I would go to dances on the weekends. I always enjoyed having a pretty girl on my arm.

I was in my last year of high school and certain I wanted to own businesses like my father and brother. I was good with my hands and thought about studying engineering, but I was more interested in owning a business instead of working for a large company.

One day, when I was walking home from working at the bakery, I noticed a For Sale sign on a mini market with a small restaurant, called the Mambo Café. The cafe had a manager, an assistant, two servers, and two cooks. It seemed like a perfect opportunity for me because it was an established cash business that needed some improvements. I knew the place well because the owner was one of our customers, so I went in to talk with him.

"Hello, Sir. How are you today? I heard you might be selling the Mambo."

"Yes, Nick," He replied. "I'm getting older, and I don't have time to pay attention to this place and keep up with my other businesses.

"How much do you want for it?" I asked.

"Does your father want to buy the Mambo?"

"No, Sir, I do," I replied.

"How old are you, Nick? You must be eighteen to sign a purchase contract or get a business license. You need to wait a few years, my boy."

"Sir, if I could make the down payment and get my parents to help with the license, would you sell it to me? You know me. I'm smart and I work hard. Plus, my father is right down the street at the bakery if I would have any problems. I know I could do this. Would you give me a chance?"

The owner and I talked a little longer and he told me the price. I'd saved up 350 British Pounds in a green metal cash box, just enough to make the down payment. There was just one problem. I was too young to make a purchase contract.

"Mama, I need your help." I asked when I arrived home. "I want to buy the Mambo Café. I have the money I need for the down payment, but I can't sign the contract or get a license without an adult signing for me. Will you sign for me, please Mama?"

"Oh, Nico, are you sure? You are only sixteen. Do you think the employees will listen to you? Owning a business is a big responsibility. You'll be responsible for lots of money, inventory, and people's jobs. What will you do if your employees steal from you or think you are too young to supervise them?"

After Mama and I talked a bit more, she said we'd discuss it with my father that evening.

After a long discussion regarding my plans and ideas, Baba said, "Son, you are a serious person and a diligent worker. If you take care of this business, I know you'll succeed. Learn fast and believe nothing is impossible for you. Nothing."

My mother finally said she would help me. She reminded me the business would be my responsibility and I would have to control it carefully so no one would take advantage of me. She advised me to work hard, pay close attention to make sure employees did not steal, and follow what I learned from my father. Then she made the sign of the Greek Orthodox cross and started to pray for my success.

With that, I had the blessings of both of my parents. I negotiated with the seller to purchase the café for a down payment and thirty-six monthly payments for the balance. It was an exciting time for me. I was finishing school, playing soccer, working in the bakery, and now had my own business. I was on the verge of the beginning of my adult life, and it was off to a thrilling start.

The first thing I did was paint the building inside and out and do a general clean-up. Then, I started to learn, ask questions, and observe.

My father's accountant advised me on controlling the inventory and managing the cash flow. I got to know the employees and asked them to share their ideas about improving the business. I would stop in to visit the store a few times each day.

My suppliers gave me a hard time. They could not believe I owned the business and said, "You're just a kid. Are you sure this isn't your father's business?"

"Yes, sir, this is my business. I am working very hard to make it a success. I'd like to keep buying things from your supply firm, but if I am to do that, you'll have to deal with me. Will that work for you?"

"Okay, kid, if you say so. I just hope you know what you are doing. As long as you pay your bill on time, your age doesn't really matter to me. Just don't miss any payments."

My school friends were amazed I owned a business. I was so busy with school, soccer, and my work at the bakery and café, the guys would come to visit me at the bakery.

One of my friends asked, "Do you really know how to work all these big machines?"

"Sure, I do," I answered. "I've been spending time in bakeries for most of my life. Someday, I might buy one of my own bakeries. You guys should think about going into business too. It's fun. I have the freedom to do whatever I want in my own business. If I want to try having a sale on a product, I do it and watch to see the results. No one tells me what to do or when to work. I'm in charge."

"Oh, Nick," another friend laughed, "you are at work all the time! Don't you want to have fun?"

"My work is fun. Plus, I still have time for everything else I want to do. I might be busy, but I'm building my future. And, I have more girls chasing me than you do!" I said as I gave him a light punch on the shoulder.

I was always trying to inspire my friends to go into business so they could control their destiny. A few of them took my advice.

I spent a lot of time and effort improving Mambo Café, first because I wanted to succeed, and second because I wanted to prove I was my own person and ready to be a business owner. My efforts paid off and I was able to complete the loan payments and keep all my suppliers' accounts current. The employees were willing to follow my instructions and glad to contribute their ideas for making the store even better. In time, I even had enough money saved to buy a car.

I was unwilling to let my age and other people's perceptions stop me from succeeding in what I now believed I was born to do.

Chapter 6: Danger on the Dirt Roads

When I got my driver's license, I started managing the bakery's deliveries. I also worked as a driver, clocking 35,000 miles each year.

Because I liked to drive and enjoy the scenery, I would often take the longest route—a round trip of 180 miles. It passed through a remote area known as the Zimba Reserve, the home of the indigenous tribes of the Shona people. Luckily, I was fluent in Shona by that time because it was the language our workers and African customers in the bakery spoke it. To me, it seemed like Greek, so I was able to learn it quickly.

Everyone worried about me driving in this area. The reserve was full of dangerous animals, including lions, leopards, hyenas, deadly black and green mamba snakes, spitting cobras, and many more. Those animals would not hesitate to see me as a tasty meal.

The area was quite different from Gatooma. People lived in mud huts, without running water or electricity. It felt as if I traveled back in time twice each week.

At that time, Rhodesia was segregated, and few whites would travel in the Zimba area because it was very remote with deplorable dirt roads. I was the only white delivery driver.

At every stop on my route, children would run up to me as if they had never seen a white face. I'd speak to them in Shona and give them a bit of bread or pastry. I had fun interacting with the shy children and making them smile.

The people in Zimba were amazed when I spoke Shona with a local accent. They called me 'Muana Murungu' in Shona, which meant young white boy. People loved my father's bread and were glad for the deliveries.

Based on the story of my father and the Nazis, I knew delicious bread could build bonds when served with respectful behavior. I treated each person I met along my routes with respect and never had any problems.

Sometimes, I would wake up feeling worried about driving this route. It was intimidating. In some areas, groups of teens hung around the stores and seemed a bit menacing. I was careful to do my job and move on quickly. It would have been easy for someone to harm me in such an isolated area. However, I luckily never had any serious problems with any people. My greatest challenges came from the combination of dirt roads and torrential rains.

When it rained, the roads were almost impassable. I had an assistant traveling with me, a full set of tools, and a few critical parts in the van at all times. I also carried a sturdy wooden club.

There were no telephones in that area in those days, so we had to be prepared to handle any problems ourselves.

My delivery van was specially modified with higher than normal suspension to drive through about three feet of water, up to the bottom of the headlights. The one-lane bridges were extremely low and often washed away or flooded during heavy rains, so the modified van allowed us to drive though rivers or flooding.

When it was raining at night on those return trips, my assistant and I would pile the empty van with large rocks to weigh it down in case we had to drive through flooded rivers, so we didn't get washed away.

I knew I could safely go through water that was up to the height of the headlights. Water might seep into the van but if it stayed under the bottom of the seats, we would be safe. We were fortunate we never were struck by logs, sank into a deep hole, or were swept away in floodwaters.

During this time, change was sweeping over the African nations north of Rhodesia, where the African population rose against the colonial rule to achieve independence. I was out on deliveries a few days following the violent attacks and the fall of the colonial government in the former Belgian Congo. The dirt roads I traveled were a shortcut from the Congo to South Africa, a 3,000-mile journey through Zambia then Rhodesia then to South Africa.

I will never forget the day I encountered a long line of large American-made cars with left-hand steering full of white people. I'd never seen such traffic in this remote area. These were white settlers fleeing murder, danger, and violence in Belgian Congo. The cars were loaded down, full of people, suitcases, and clothing. Some had boxes and bundles piled on the roof. I saw car after car filled with haunted faces on that narrow dirt road. It was clear this was not a group on a vacation, but people escaping from something horrible.

The newspapers we read at home had been filled with accounts of colonial settlers leaving their homes, businesses, and belongings behind, making a desperate journey out of Belgian Congo to South Africa. Now, I saw some of these people on the road in front of me. I never forgot the sight of those frightened families.

Rhodesia had a stable government. However, some of the African population, especially in remote areas, started expressing an interest in underground politics centered around the African population gaining power from the white population.

Some of the politically minded store owners in Zimba would not buy bread from me unless I was a member of the underground independence movement, the Zimbabwe African Peoples Union (ZAPU).

If the Rhodesian authorities discovered my affiliation with ZAPU, I knew I would face stiff consequences, probably jail. However, I was not permitted to sell bread without a card. I decided to purchase a membership in ZAPU under an assumed name. Once I had my membership card, I was able to sell bread and pastries to all the stores in Zimba.

I heard a few racist remarks from shop owners who shouted at me and said I wasn't welcome in the store because I was white. Whenever I had problems at a particular location, I would not argue. I would just leave and remove that store from my route. Most of the people were happy to see me, though, especially since I spoke their language and treated everyone with respect, as my parents taught me.

When I was delivering in the Zimba reserve one day, the ground was very muddy from heavy rain the day before. We were close to the end of our route, about eighty-five miles from Gatooma. My assistant and I pulled into a dirt parking area in front of a store to unload our delivery. Once I completed the transaction and collected the cash, I went back to the van and discovered it was sunk deep into the soft mud, up to the floor, reaching the bottom of the doors. There was no way to drive out of that mud or pull the van out with just two men.

"Do you need some help?"

I heard a deep voice speaking to me in English, turned and saw a man walking towards the van. The first thing I noticed about him was his eyes, they were unusually bright.

I replied, "Yes, Sir. We are really stuck in the mud. I have ropes, flashlights, and tools in the van, but we can't get this out by ourselves.

"Do not worry," the man said. "I will bring some men and cows from the village to pull you out."

While we waited, I started to think of my parents and how worried they would be if I did not return home that night. They knew I had a great deal of money in the van after a full day of deliveries. There were no telephones in the area, so I could not call them. I was not afraid, but I did not want to worry my parents.

Thirty minutes later, the gentleman returned with a group of men and two cattle. We tied the truck with ropes, and then put the cows and men all around the vehicle. I got in, started the engine, and asked everyone if they were ready. I slowly released the clutch, careful not to rev the engine, which would have spun the tires, splashed mud all over the people helping, and sunk the van deeper in the mud. Slowly, the van began to move as everyone worked together.

When the van got to dry ground, the entire group broke out in a cheer. I went to each man, shook his hand, and thanked him. My helper and I gave everyone some bread and a bit of money as a reward. When I got to the man with the bright eyes, I said, "My name is Nick. Thank you very much for helping us today."

"I know who you are," he replied. "I am Robert. I teach at the school here. We will see each other again."

When I returned to that shop later that week with more deliveries, Robert was waiting for me. He asked for me to give him a ride. The bakery policy said not to take passengers in our vans, but since he'd helped me, I felt it was only right to return the favor.

He spoke in fluent English and appeared to be more educated than other people from the area. When we talked, I was reminded of a professor, as he made his points quickly and concisely.

Robert's eyes were unusual, large, and sparkling. I noticed his eyes every time I saw him because they were so bright and constantly looking around. It seemed strange he was so vigilant. I wondered if he did not want anyone to see him.

While we were driving, we talked. "Robert, you said you were a teacher. Do you enjoy your students?" I asked.

"Yes, Nick. I believe education is vitally important. I am here to teach and to help people," Robert said.

"What kind of help? I asked.

"I am giving people knowledge so they can be independent." After that remark, Robert was silent for the rest of the ride. He seemed very mysterious at that moment.

Over the following months, Robert asked me for many rides. I always agreed. None of the rides were too long. I'd just drop him where he wanted to go in Zimba. We had many conversations and began to seem like friends. I enjoyed talking with him, even though he was about twenty-five years older than me. He was knowledgeable, well-spoken, and able to discuss many different topics.

However, I always noticed how carefully he chose his words, especially when discussing politics. He told me he'd graduated from a nearby school run by Catholic missionaries, Koutama Mission, where he learned English. He was careful about what he said, which made me cautious about sharing too much of my life and opinions as well.

After some time, I lost track of Robert. I began to take on more management duties at the bakery and stopped driving the long route to Zimba Reserve, turning it over to another driver, but I never forgot Robert and his kindness when I really needed it.

Chapter 7: High Stakes Negotiation

As soon as I graduated from high school, I decided to buy another business. I found a trading store with a meat market called Ngezi Trading, located in one of the suburbs of Gatooma. This store was larger than Mambo Café with three sections: groceries, meats, and clothing. It featured a prime location on a large suburb's main road and had a big parking lot. It also had a full staff, which I liked because I didn't have to start from scratch, recruit, and hire people.

After I purchased it, I painted, cleaned, and improved the parking lot to attract more customers. Next, I instituted the control system I devised at Mambo Cafe to prevent theft and streamline processes. I also asked employees for suggestions on improvements and implemented their best ideas. This business was easier to run and more profitable because it sold many ready-made products with a significant markup.

By the time I was eighteen, I felt on top of the world. I had a fast car, nice clothes, and plenty of good friends. My businesses were doing well, and I got a lot of attention from playing on the city soccer team. I was studying engineering via correspondence courses, which I found fascinating. However, there was something brewing under the surface that nagged at me.

"The bakery has cash flow problems." Cathreen told me one night.

"That can't be right!" I replied. "Baba makes the best bread in 100 kilometers, maybe even the best bread in all of Rhodesia. Plus, we've spent years streamlining operations and expanding our market reach. Everyone in Gatooma knows our bakery. You can't go to a store in Gatooma and not find our products on the shelves."

"That's all true, Nico, but look at these figures." Cathreen was studying accounting and had taken over the bookkeeping at the bakery. She started showing me the account ledgers. "See here, this is a list of fifteen customers who have not paid their bills in six months! We keep giving them product and they get to keep the money they owe us for months. Did you know we are paying a big commission on every bag of flour, sugar, and yeast? What is Baba doing?"

"Have you asked him about this, Cathreen?" I replied.

"It's very strange. He doesn't want to discuss money with me. He just said he was taking care of his friends and wasn't worried about money. His words were, 'We make the best bread in the world. Why should we worry about money?' I was shocked. These accounts show me we should be worrying about money. Even though we are busier than ever, we are not making any more profit. In fact, profits decreased from last year. Baba doesn't want to admit it, but something needs to change here."

This was the first of many conversations Cathreen and I had about the bakery. We'd both been working there part-time ever since we moved to Gatooma, for more than eight years. We did not receive a salary, but we both lived at home and had all our living expenses covered, so that seemed fair. Peter lived at home, too, and was busy with his stores, but he'd never been interested in working at the bakery, so we could not discuss the problem with him. In fact, he was one of the customers who were not paying their bills on time.

I decided to see if Baba would listen to my ideas as he had in the past.

"Baba, I think we should start replacing some of the machinery. It's getting old. Plus, there are newer machines that would help us modernize. What do you think?"

"Oh, Nico, what we have now is working fine. Let's just keep things as they are for a while." Baba replied.

When I told Cathreen, we started to question our future.

"Sister, what do you want to do? Do you want to keep working in the bakery, or devote more time to your dressmaking? I bet you would make a good living if you got your own store downtown instead of sewing at home," I implored.

"I don't know, Nico. It doesn't seem like the bakery is going to last very long if Baba keeps ignoring the finances. What will he and Mama do if they lose it? They've worked so hard."

"That's true," I replied. "But what about us? We are adults now, Cathreen. We can't keep working for free forever. Plus, we're both frustrated Baba doesn't want to listen to our ideas. He's changed. He doesn't want to grow anymore. I can't sit by and watch him destroy the bakery. What would happen if we left?"

Cathreen drew in a sharp breath. "I never imagined leaving the bakery until I got married. What would that do to our family? I don't want to hurt Baba and Mama. They've done so much for us, leaving behind everyone they loved in Greece so we could have a future."

It seemed as if Cathreen and I had the same discussion every day for months as we tried to find a solution that would not harm our parents and still give us the opportunity to grow our own careers. Finally, we came up with the idea of buying the bakery from our father so he could retire and enjoy life more.

First, we had a conversation with Mama. It was difficult, but Mama listened intently as we told her Baba seemed to be losing his enthusiasm for the bakery and no longer interested in growth and expansion.

"Well, my children," she said, "it is true your father is becoming tired. He has worked extremely hard for many years. I know his back hurts and it is getting harder for him to do any lifting or stand on his feet for long hours. He is a proud man and will not want his children to say he is failing or not giving the bakery enough attention. If you want to buy the bakery from him, talk about all he's taught you and you feel ready to carry on in the family tradition. I do not know what he will say, but please, have a discussion with him before you decide to leave the bakery."

The next evening, Cathreen and I presented a business case for the bakery, stressing how we wanted to see it grow and felt ready to use the lessons we'd learned watching our father guide the bakery for the last eight years. He agreed to think about our offer for a few days.

Finally, he agreed to sell us the bakery, and Cathreen and I became co-owners of the bakery in 1969. We were very excited. Mama and Baba were supportive and gave us suggestions around the dinner table, but we were careful not to depend on them too much. It was our time to succeed now.

Cathreen worked on organizing the financial reports and other administrative tasks. My first job was to negotiate with my father's friends to pay off their balances and adjust to new terms. There were about fifteen of these accounts.

It was a delicate situation, as these men were my father's best friends. Most were from Greece. My father served as the best man at one of these men's wedding's and was the godfather to another's son. They'd known our family for years. Unfortunately, they'd seen

Cathreen and I grow up and still viewed us as youngsters, not as business owners. I had to make a bold move.

I visited each man in his office and asked for a payment plan to bring accounts current and begin paying for their purchases within fifteen days of receiving their monthly invoice. None of the men were happy about this. Some accused me of being a fool who did not know what he was doing. Others tried to appeal to the friendship between our families. A few told me I was a poor businessman and would never succeed.

During these discussions, I stayed calm. I explained we had to build up our cash flow for the bakery to survive. We were not a bank and were changing our practices to match other bakeries' norms in Rhodesia. I was respectful yet determined.

Because I knew them well, I knew most of them had multiple stores and were able to pay. They had money and did not need the bakery to be a loan agency. That information gave me confidence.

Some of the men reluctantly agreed, and we negotiated solutions. A few canceled their orders and began buying from our competition. I held firm and insisted on the new payment terms. I was confident in our product, which was superior to any other bread available. I was willing to gamble their customers would complain about inferior quality from other suppliers.

Slowly but surely, this gamble paid off. In time, they all returned to us after their bread sales dropped and customers complained. All the outstanding balances were paid, immediately improving cash flow.

Next, I had to negotiate with my older brother, Peter. At that time, there was a large warehouse on the bakery lot. Peter and I would go to factories and negotiate a bulk purchase of their overruns. For example, we'd purchase ten thousand bars of soap, store them in the warehouse and later, sell them at all our stores at low prices designed to attract shoppers. The bakery paid for the warehouse, including inventory control, and loading and unloading all the freight. Peter never paid any fees for his storage in the warehouse, or the labor required to load and unload his freight. Peter's accounts with the bakery were also past due.

"Peter, we need to talk about your overdue balance at the bakery. We have a new policy now that all commercial payments are due in thirty days, not six months. Would you like to set up a payment plan to bring your stores' accounts up to date easily? We also need to talk about the warehouse. Cathreen and I are happy for you to continue to use the free storage, but we think it is fair for you to contribute to the labor costs when you use the bakery vans to move merchandise to your stores. Let's talk about a fair price."

"Are you crazy, Nico?" Peter exploded. "I'm part of this family. The bakery and warehouse are part of our family business. Of course, I should be able to use them."

"Brother, the bakery is no longer our family business. Cathreen and I used our own money to buy it from Baba, you know that. Your stores are separate from the bakery and always have been. In that respect, you are a customer of the bakery and must be treated like we treat all our customers."

"That is nonsense, Nico! The bakery belongs to our family and that means me too. You and Cathreen are just being greedy. I'm going to start buying my bread from another bakery." Peter fumed and left the room.

Peter and I barely spoke for a week. Whenever I tried to reason with him, he just became angrier. Everyone in the family felt the strain. We'd always been close friends and brothers. Now it felt like Peter was on one side of a deep ravine while Cathreen and I stood on the other. We could not figure out how to bridge the gap between us.

Finally, Mama sat the three of us down for a stern lecture. "This has gone on long enough. We are a family and that is more important than money or business. You know that—all three of you. Peter, that bakery pays for every bit of your life, the food you eat, the bed you sleep in, everything you have here at this house. The money Cathreen and Nico paid your father for the bakery is still paying for your life and it will for as long as you live under this roof. The bakery belongs to Nico and Cathreen now and you must respect that.

"Now, I want you to all remember you love each other. Peter, you must be fair. Let your business pay just like all the others do. You have enough money to pay your bills on time. I imagine you must pay your other suppliers in thirty days. Is that not true?"

"Yes, Mama," Peter sheepishly agreed.

"Then why would you expect to treat your own family worse than you treat a stranger?" Mama asked.

"You are right, Mama." Peter admitted. "Nico, Cathreen, I am sorry. I want you to succeed with the bakery. In fact, I'm proud you bought it. I'll do my part and make sure my stores follow your new payment policy."

Now that I'd tackled the problems with my father's cronies and my brother, there was one other difficult negotiation I had to undertake, one that would bring the bakery 120,000 dollars in additional profits each year if I was successful, which was a large sum of money at the time. However, if I failed, I would alienate the most powerful man in Gatooma and our primary supplier and biggest customer.

Samuel Hasson was the richest and most influential man in Gatooma. Also from Greece, he owned most of the businesses in the city, as well as factories and vast farms. The mayor, police, judges, bank managers, politicians, and other influential people respected Mr. Hasson and sought his advice. He was also a friend of my family who gave Peter his first job and helped my father establish himself in Gatooma.

Our businesses were intricately linked. Mr. Hasson purchased our bakery products. The bakery purchased sugar, oil, paper, and other supplies from his business. Mr. Hasson also brokered a deal with the milling company for our flour, which earned him an eight percent commission on every truckload of flour we purchased.

My father, Peter, and I also periodically purchased items for our stores from Mr. Hasson. However, I realized we were overpaying on all our supplies because we relied on Mr. Hasson to act as a middleman. I knew we would save a fortune by working directly with manufacturers and convincing Mr. Hasson to pay for his bakery purchases.

Because Mr. Hasson was so powerful and influential, negotiating with him required much thought and planning. Cathreen and I discussed things carefully, then I made an appointment to meet with Mr. Hasson in his office.

Some would find a meeting like this daunting and fear failing to get Mr. Hasson's agreement. I don't fear failure, instead I see failure as a learning experience. I did my homework and prepared carefully for the meeting, gathering all the facts and figures. I was ready to go into battle and knew I could win.

When I entered Mr. Hasson's office, I began by talking about how much I admired his success and position in our city. I thanked him for all the help he'd given to our family and me personally. Then, I discussed our new payment policies and that I did not want to go behind his back slyly, but I planned to approach the milling companies directly and negotiate my own deals so he would no longer receive his flour commission.

"Nico Haritatos, what do you think you are doing? You are a brash young man who moves too fast and will certainly fail," Mr. Hasson sputtered.

He called his manager to join the meeting, and now I was faced with two powerful men who were much older than I was. It was intimidating, yet something in my gut was telling me not to give up and go home empty-handed. If only I could find a way of keeping them from exploding and throwing me out of the office.

Carefully, and with great respect, I reminded them I came to the meeting with honesty and in the spirit of transparency. I did not want to approach the milling companies without their knowledge, although I might have, because of our extended family friendship. I thanked Mr. Hasson again for all the ways he'd helped us establish the bakery and begin our life in Gatooma.

"Mr. Hasson, my family loves you and wants to maintain our long friendship and business relationship. I admire you very much and want to follow in your footsteps as a successful businessman. The only way I can save the bakery is if I make these changes, increase production and profitability. I will work day and night to pull the bakery out of this hole.

"When you came to Rhodesia from Greece, you were like me. You were a young and ambitious man who had to take risks to climb to a higher level. This undertaking is a big risk for me, but I have no other choice."

He looked at me for a long time, saying nothing. The manager was silent. Finally, Mr. Hasson said, "Nick, a commercial bakery is a complicated and difficult business. You are so young. How are you going to manage that responsibility as well as take care of your stores?"

I quickly replied, "Hard work, Mr. Hasson."

He was quiet for another time, then said, "Okay, Nick, I admire your guts and spirit. I am not happy about this, but I will support you. I'll call the milling companies and tell them you are coming to negotiate with them directly. I will also follow your new policy and pay my bills in thirty days. But you must know, I'll be watching closely to see if you can handle all these responsibilities."

We shook hands, and I left his office greatly relieved. The negotiation was incredibly stressful, and I was proud I hadn't cracked under pressure. I achieved the outcome the bakery needed. If it had gone badly, Mr. Hasson had the power to ruin my reputation in Gatooma, but because I was respectful and approached him before I talked to the milling companies, he saw I meant him no harm, even though it cost him money. I'd found a way to negotiate with the most powerful man in the city and maintain a good relationship. A heavy weight rolled off my shoulders as I drove back to the bakery to share the good news with Cathreen.

Mr. Hasson was true to his word. He continued to be one of our biggest customers and paid his bills on time. Every now and then, Mr. Hasson would visit me in the bakery to check on our progress. I'd show him new equipment and some of the changes we were making. I admired him greatly and wanted to prove my worth as a businessman.

In time, he told me I was doing a good job. Even now, that compliment makes my heart swell with pride. I'd learned the secret of negotiation: to be well prepared and respectful, but never to be intimidated by someone who believed they were superior to me. Because I was not afraid of failing, I met Mr. Hasson as an equal, businessman to businessman.

Chapter 8: Two Become One

A few years before Cathreen and I purchased the bakery, I'd met Anne, a lovely, blue-eyed, dark-haired beauty from South Africa. Her mother was a new physician in Gatooma, and Anne was visiting while she was on a break from her university in Johannesburg. As soon as I met her, I was struck by her intelligence, lovely speaking voice, and kindness. There was something special about her.

After that day, I thought about Anne constantly and how I could see her again without her phone number or address. I considered knocking on all the doors in the neighborhood, but that seemed silly. Then, I thought of the municipal swimming pool. It was December and extremely hot. Perhaps she would be taking her younger siblings to the municipal pool on a warm afternoon.

One day, I was lucky enough to drive near the pool and see Anne and her five siblings—four little sisters and a brother. I drove up and asked them if they would like a ride home.

"Oh, no thanks, Nick. We'll get your nice car all dirty," Anne told me.

I had to hold back a smile when one of her little sisters piped up saying she was tired and would love a ride home. Everyone climbed in my car, and I drove them home, glad to realize they lived only five blocks from my house. The trip was over much too quickly, though.

I was determined to ask Anne for a date but still didn't know her number. Later that night, I looked up all the doctors in the phone book and found a listing for her mother. I called the number and asked to speak to Anne.

"This is Nick. Would you like to go to the movies with me?"

Anne replied. "No, thank you. I must leave to go back to Johannesburg in a few weeks."

Then I could hear her mother in the background. "Who's on the phone?"

Anne must have covered up the speaker on the phone as her voice was muffled. "Some boy wants to take me to the movies."

"Who is he?" her mother's muffled voice asked.

"He is the son of the baker who lives in the neighborhood," Anne replied.

"Oh, you should go. I know that baker. He is a nice man with a good family."

Anne came back on the line, saying she wasn't sure.

"Come on, Anne, it will be fun." I begged. You can bring your sister. In fact, you can bring all four of your sisters. Just come to the movies with me."

Anne finally agreed to go the movies with me, and after that one date, I knew she would be my wife in the future. We quickly became inseparable.

However, she had to return to South Africa to her university, so we began a tradition of writing letters back and forth. We wrote each other every day. I didn't like writing letters or have much spare time, but I was happy to write to Anne.

While we waited for her next university break, we shared all the events of our lives as well as our hopes and dreams for the future in our letters. We discussed everything.

I was always impressed by Anne's quick mind. She loved hearing about my stores and the bakery and asked many wise questions. Even though she was studying to become a physician, like her mother, she had a keen grasp of business.

Each time she came to Gatooma, we learned more about each other. I'd visit her family, which was very different from mine. Her mother was a very busy doctor who made house calls, so she was gone often seeing her patients. Anne, as the eldest, took care of her younger siblings. She was so kind and attentive to them I knew she'd be a wonderful mother to any children we might have in the future.

Anne's mother was of Dutch descent, a descendant of the early South African settlers who spoke Afrikaans. Her father was of Irish decent, a mining engineer and a very tough, stern man. He never seemed to warm up to me, although I was always very respectful. I wondered if he wanted Anne to date someone who attended college or came from a wealthier family.

Luckily, Anne's mother really liked me and advocated for our relationship, encouraging Anne to consider another career so she would have more time with her family in the future.

My parents loved Anne, as well. She was so sweet and kind people warmed up to her as soon as they met her. After dating for a year or so, Anne and I were committed to marrying as soon as she completed her education. She decided to follow her mother's advice and change her course of study to Psychology instead of Medicine.

My parents were very conservative and taught me marriage was forever, and I had to choose a wife who would encourage me, be a good mother, and always be on my side. I found all those qualities in Anne. I was her idol, and she was mine. Anne inspired me to dream big and to grow. I was determined to be successful and provide a beautiful life for her and the children we would have together someday.

In time, I started visiting her in South Africa, meeting her many relatives there—several uncles and their families. Her Auntie Poppie and Uncle Willem became very close to us, hosting us in their home often when I was visiting. Auntie Poppie and Uncle Willem became like second parents to Anne while she was in South Africa and welcomed me into their family with open arms.

When Anne was in Gatooma, she'd visit me in the bakery or my stores, asking questions about everything. We loved to go out dancing as often as possible. She loved dancing just as much as I did.

By 1970, after dating for almost five years, we could not wait any longer to marry. However, our situation was complicated because of the laws of South Africa and the traditions of my Greek Orthodox Church. We had two weddings, both in South Africa since Anne was a citizen there. The first was a tiny civil ceremony where we were married in the eyes of the government.

I picked up Anne, her sister, and a few of her friends from the university, we drove to the registry office, and were soon legally wed. After a tiny celebration in a nearby park, I had to take Anne back to school for her afternoon classes.

"Goodbye, Mrs. Haritatos," I told her as I dropped her off on campus.

"Goodbye, Husband. I'll be home soon." Anne laughed.

We were thrilled to be legally married, even though I needed to return to Gatooma in a few days to get back to the bakery. It was hard to part, but we knew we had to stick with our plan until Anne's graduation.

While I was back in Rhodesia, I considered what to buy her for a special wedding present. I wrote her one day and asked about what kind of a car she'd like to have. When Anne replied she'd always loved the look of a red Jaguar, I knew just what I wanted to buy for my sweetie. She looked beautiful behind the wheel of that fast red car. I glowed with pride to know my hard work enabled me to purchase it for her. I wanted to give her the whole world and promised myself I'd work as hard to build her a beautiful life.

Anne graduated with her master's degree in Psychology in 1971. I was so proud of my beautiful and accomplished wife. Shortly after, we had a beautiful church wedding in the Greek Orthodox Cathedral in Pretoria, South Africa. It was a wonderful affair. Auntie Poppie arranged everything for us, just as if she were Anne's mother. Our families gathered from all over Rhodesia and South Africa to celebrate our marriage and consecrate it in the eyes of God.

After the wedding, we embarked on a six-week honeymoon trip to Europe, beginning our journey in London. Neither of us were accustomed to international travel, so we felt like innocents when we arrived in such a large and sophisticated city.

"Oh Nick, I left my purse in the taxi!" Anne exclaimed one evening as we returned to our hotel. "Our passports, traveler's cheques, and my engagement ring was in there. Oh, the hotel key was in there too! What are we going to do?" Anne began to cry, and I took her in my arms out on the sidewalk.

"My sweetheart, do not cry. We will find a way. Let's begin with the hotel."

"Nick, we don't have our money, just the little bit in your wallet. How are we going to pay our bill?"

"I don't know yet, Darling. Let's take things one step at a time. We can figure this out."

We went inside and spoke to the hotel clerk who was very helpful. He gave us a duplicate key for our room and advised us to visit our embassies to apply for duplicate passports the following morning. It was a long night. We held each other and cried from the stress and worry.

Things looked a little brighter the following morning. I was able to get a new passport at the Greek embassy. When we went to the South African embassy, we learned Anne needed a South African citizen to testify to her identity. Thankfully, Anne's sister had just arrived in London. She met us at the embassy, loaned us a little money, and soon, Anne had a passport.

We continued to explore London but had to limit our excursions to conserve our money. In a stroke of luck, three days later, the hotel staff told us the police called and had Anne's handbag at the station. The cab driver had turned it in. Everything was there—our passports, money, and traveler's cheques, which seemed like a miracle. The only thing missing was Anne's engagement ring.

"Nick, I am just heartbroken about my ring. I loved it so much because you gave it to me as a symbol of our love. I am so sorry it is gone. It's all my fault."

"My darling wife, everything is alright. I'll get you another ring when we go home. We're safe and have everything we need. As long as you are with me, I am a happy man," I reassured Anne.

While that experience was scary, it taught us we could work together well during a crisis.

Later during our trip, I took Anne to Greece. I had not been there since we left for Rhodesia. What a thrill it was to see the place of my birth and my relatives! I was proud to introduce Anne to my family and friends who celebrated our visit. My heart was full of joy to see my loved ones and the warm welcome they gave to Anne.

We had a wonderful time exploring Greece, visiting the Parthenon and other historic sites. How happy I felt the day Anne and I went to Olympia and ran around the track at the site of the Ancient Olympic games, just as I'd done years ago with Baba and Peter.

During our time in Greece, I opened a bank account at my father's recommendation. He felt it was wise for me to have an account in Europe. He was concerned about the political unrest brewing in northern Rhodesia and believed I should store some funds outside the country.

When we returned from our honeymoon, Anne's parents had moved to Salisbury from Gatooma, so we rented their house and set about making it our own.

As soon as I returned to the bakery, Cathreen said, "Nick, Mama wants to have an official meeting with us."

"Do you know why?" I asked.

"No, I can't guess. Things are going great here at the bakery, thanks to all the new equipment and systems we put in. We're making more bread and larger profits than ever before. I'm going to finish my accounting degree this semester and she's very glad you and Anne are married. It's very mysterious," Cathreen replied.

Later that day, Mama came to the bakery office to talk to us. "Children," she said, "I am very proud of all the work you've done at the bakery. However, I am worried about your father. Ever since he sold the bakery, he's been bored. He doesn't have enough to do at home or with his store. His life seems empty to him if he isn't baking bread. Would you consider selling the bakery back to him? You don't need to answer me now. Just think it over."

Cathreen and I had a long discussion after Mama left. On one hand, we'd worked so hard to improve the bakery it didn't seem right to walk away once it was running smoothly. On the other hand, we'd both enjoyed the process of improving things so much our current situation felt a bit stale and routine.

Finally, Cathreen said. "Here's the most important question for us to consider. Do we want to stay in Gatooma and run this bakery for the rest of our lives?"

At that moment, I realized if we sold the bakery, I'd be free to go anywhere with Anne and start a new life together, out of the shadows of our families. As much as I loved my family, perhaps it was time for us to strike out on our own and build something together.

That evening, Anne and I had a long talk about our future. We both became very excited about the possibility of starting over with something new. Neither of us felt content to stay in Gatooma when we had so many other options. It was fun to dream about the places we might go. Anne loved South Africa and had always dreamed of moving to Durban, a beautiful city on the coast. There were also many opportunities in Rhodesia since the business environment there was less established. We went to sleep that night brimming over with ideas and goals. After working and waiting for five years to marry, selling the bakery would give us enough money to go anywhere and establish a business together.

At the bakery the next morning, Cathreen and I both agreed we had to sell the bakery back to Baba. He'd sacrificed so much for us and worked so hard to provide for us. Cathreen was just as ready to leave Gatooma as Anne and I were, so it was really no hardship for either of us. We also decided it would be right to sell the bakery back to our father for the same price we'd paid for it. We didn't feel comfortable making a profit from our parents.

In a few weeks, we completed the sale. Baba was delighted to return to his passion for baking the best bread in Gatooma. Cathreen completed her degree and secured a very good job working in at the police headquarters of Salisbury as an accountant.

Anne and I felt as if the world were our oyster. We were young, full of love for each other, and had a solid nest egg to establish a new business. It was time to decide on our next adventure.

Chapter 9: The Crown of Rhodesia

Anne and I did extensive research into a variety of business ideas. Based on our long courtship conducted via letter writing, we knew each other well and that we wanted the same things: freedom, flexibility, family time, and fun. I loved the autonomy of owning my own business. Anne and I shared a passion for growth and achievement. We also loved change.

"Sweetie, do you want to continue living in Gatooma? We could go anywhere if we sold the Mambo and Ngezi Trading," I asked during one of our long discussions over dinner.

"What if we tried someplace new? I'd like to see what we might build in a place where no one knew our parents. I'll always be 'the doctor's daughter' here and you'll be 'the bakery owner's son' in this town."

Anne was right. It was exciting to think of starting over in a new community. Because I'd moved several times already, I had a system for establishing myself in a new location: find a soccer team, make some friends, then find a need in that community.

I'd watched my father succeed in Rhodesia because he was skilled at making friends and baking bread everyone enjoyed. I didn't want to be a baker, but we could find another need to fill. We were so committed to moving I sold the Mambo Café and my other store so we would be free to move whenever the time was right.

After some research, we decided to open a drive-in theater. Drive-ins were new and immensely popular at the time, especially for families. There were very few drive-ins located in Rhodesia, so this was a hot opportunity. Plus, we both thought it would be a fun business we could do together. Anne and I began to research and plan our strategy.

First, we identified the cities in Rhodesia that had a population able to support a drive-in. We selected three cities as our top choices, then visited them. The best opportunity was in Fort Victoria, where the city planners had just completed a 15-acre parcel of land, close to the city center, for a drive-in and were ready to accept bids.

We liked Fort Victoria. It was in the southern part of Rhodesia, two hundred miles from the border, making it easy for us to visit Anne's relatives in South Africa regularly. The city was popular with tourists who came to tour the Zimbabwe Ruins, an ancient stone complex, so there were many hotels and restaurants. It was also near a large dam at Lake Kyle, offering water sports, beaches, and parks. Fort Victoria had a vibrant feel full of youth and possibility.

I was impressed with the business community. There was a Coca Cola bottling factory, a large meat packing factory, an airport with daily flights from the capital, a college, hospitals, army battalion, and many large ranches in the surrounding countryside. Fort Victoria's economy was booming. We figured between the tourists, soldiers, college students, and the local population, there would be plenty of people to buy tickets for a drive-in movie.

I learned Rainbow Cinemas, a large company that owned twelve other cinemas and drive-ins in Rhodesia, was also placing a bid for the land in Fort Victoria. I investigated and discovered they had a reputation for building cheap buildings with second-hand projection equipment. Distributors did not want to give them new movie releases because their old equipment would damage and scratch the new films. This information was just what we needed for a winning bid.

Anne and I decided we'd offer Fort Victoria a luxury drive-in which would draw visitors and contribute to the city's glowing reputation, with the most modern equipment and newest films.

Anne and I got to work learning everything about drive-in theatres. We made several trips to South Africa to look at successful drive-ins there. We'd visit Auntie Poppie and Uncle Willem on most of our travels, spending the night at their home. They were always happy to see us and listen to our plans.

Our most successful trip was to Johannesburg, where we met with the three largest film distributors in the country. The meetings were very fruitful. All three distributors gave us suggestions for South African companies that would supply and install all the equipment we needed.

Drive-ins were so new in Rhodesia, that no equipment was produced there. The distributors were eager to expand into Rhodesia, so each of them agreed to supply us with a letter stating they would supply our theatre in Fort Victoria with "A-circuit" new release movies. Anne believed these letters would strengthen our bid.

While we toured the most successful drive-ins and cinemas in Johannesburg, Anne and I became more and more excited. I was very interested in the sound systems and projection equipment.

Anne noticed differences between the way different theatres handled ticket sales and concessions.

We drove home from Johannesburg, full of excitement. We hired an architect and told him we wanted to design the most innovative drive-in in Rhodesia. Our concept was based on a crown, a round two-story building, that would include outdoor seating for about eighty people with both a restaurant and bar flanking the sides of the building. No other drive-in we'd seen included a bar, but Anne and I believed patrons would enjoy having a cocktail during intermission.

Our architect drew up preliminary plans for the large lot. Because we had so much space to play with, we added space for a children's playground, a soccer field for community use during the day, parking for 800 cars, apartments for staff, and a large home for Anne and me. We also added in space for 850 pine trees, planted to surround and beautify the property. Our complex would be called the Coronet Drive-In Cinema.

Anne and I worked for hours on my pitch presentation for the Fort Victoria city council. We wrote a full script and I practiced it until I was able to recite it perfectly and confidently. Anne would listen and ask me questions to mimic being in front of an audience.

Finally, the day arrived for my presentation before the city council.

"Sweetie, they loved everything!" I exclaimed as I returned to our hotel room later that afternoon. "They were thrilled about getting the latest movies and that we were willing to invest in expensive projection and sound equipment. They also liked the idea of the soccer field so the property could be used during the day. But the idea they liked the most was the bar! They got all excited about being the first Rhodesian drive-in with a bar." I picked up Anne and swung her around in my arms. We were so happy and excited about the possibilities ahead of us.

A few weeks later, we learned we won the bid. Anne and I moved into action. First, we found a house to rent and moved in. I joined the city's professional soccer team, and we became friends with many people in Fort Victoria. The community welcomed us because everyone was very interested in our project. The newspaper did a story on the new Coronet Drive-In Cinema, generating a great deal of excitement in the community.

For the next eighteen months, we focused on construction. Anne and I decided to wait to have children for a few years so we could both put all our energy into making the drive-in a success. It was a massive project and we enjoyed adding in as many creative touches as we could. We purchased the best quality sound system available, along with a music license that would allow us to play the latest popular music.

Next, we turned our attention to operations. Anne used to joke I must have been a field marshal for Alexander the Great in a past life because I created a plan for every aspect of the drive-in. We worked together to manage all the business aspects from ticket sales to traffic flow, scheduling, food and beverage services, and marketing. I also learned how to operate and maintain the large projection machines and sound system.

The restaurant and bar posed the greatest challenge. Intermission was only twenty minutes, and we had to serve up to 300 chicken dinners each night, as well as the other meals. The bar also had to prepare and serve a vast number of drinks during that short time, as well.

My bakery and restaurant experience helped me create systems and processes to satisfy the great demand in such a short window. We spent a great deal of time training our staff of twenty-five to provide exquisite customer service so every guest would feel like royalty at the Coronet.

By mid-1972, the Coronet was ready for opening. Anne and I hosted a huge gala on opening night, inviting the mayor, city council, police, military and other business leaders to bring their wives and celebrate with us.

Moments before the party began, Anne and I stood looking at what we'd created. The glass and steel futuristic building were sparking under lights, music filled the air, and the smells of popcorn and delicious food wafted in the breeze.

As I gazed at Anne in her beautiful gown, my heart was filled with pride and wonder.

"We did it, my darling." I said as I pulled my lovely wife into my arms for a quick kiss. "Look what we built. This is our dream, and we made it real."

The next few months felt magical. Our drive-in was extremely popular. Anne managed all the movie ticketing, promotions, and marketing, and I took charge of the bar, restaurant, and projection. Every night we'd dress up and welcome patrons into our beautiful establishment. We loved working together and found we were a very good team.

"Nico, this looks like a spaceship," my father exclaimed as I gave him a tour of the projection room. Mama and Baba came from Gatooma to see the Coronet and visit us. "I thought the bakery was a complicated business. I don't know how you can manage everything you have here. It's incredible."

"Well, Baba, I only have one problem. I can't get good bread! I think you and Mama need to move to Fort Victoria and open a bakery. Nobody here can bake like you do."

My father laughed, then his face grew serious. "Nico, you've built something wonderful here. I am incredibly proud of you. I'm also worried. War is coming to Rhodesia; I know the signs. Sure, the newspapers say the guerilla attacks on the northern border are nothing to worry about, but I've been through two wars and know differently."

"Baba, do you really think so?" I asked.

"Yes, my son. War will come here, just as it has in the countries north of us. Africa is changing. Remember what happened in Belgian Congo? I want you to watch carefully, but more importantly you must prepare a safety net. Listen carefully. Do not invest all your money in this business. Save some of your capital and keep it safe. Anne is a citizen of South Africa. The government there is much stronger than ours in Rhodesia. Be smart and open a bank account there. I hope you never have to use it, but a wise man has a safety net."

After my parents returned home, I told Anne about my father's advice.

"Nick, my father believes the opposite of yours. He feels Rhodesia is strong and will continue under the current government for years. In fact, he wants to buy a gold mine near Gatooma. Who should we believe?"

After a long discussion, Anne and I decided it would not harm us to establish a safety net in South Africa since we wanted to move there eventually.

Years earlier, when we were dating, I set up a bank account there and purchased four small lots in a residential development in Pretoria because Uncle Willem believed they would be a wise investment.

Auntie Poppie and Uncle Willem recently moved to Phalaborwa, in northeast South Africa, near Kruger National Park. We decided to take a trip to see them. They were always glad to see us and listened carefully to our concerns about the future of Rhodesia.

Willem suggested we consider investing in Phalaborwa, since it was a growing city but lacked a strong retail community. As we drove around the city, I noticed few national brand stores, only locally owned businesses.

"What if I built a shopping center here?" I mused.

Willem said, "Nick, that is a terrific idea! This town needs a shopping center, and it is only a matter of time before somebody builds one. Why not you?"

Uncle Willem connected us with a commercial real estate broker, and we toured possible sites for a mall. We found a place with an excellent location and made a bold offer. The all-cash offer had to be accepted or declined within forty-eight hours. I offered a significant down payment, which I agreed to forfeit if I did not pay off the balance in five months. I planned to sell at least three of the four residential lots in Pretoria and use the money for this commercial property together with other cash I'd stored in South Africa.

This strategy was risky. Due to the UN sanctions against Rhodesia, I was not allowed to move much currency out of the country, even though I'd earned it legally and paid taxes on it, so I had to use funds that were already in South Africa. I believed I could sell the lots in Pretoria at a price that would cover the purchase, so we took the risk.

Thankfully, the lots in Pretoria sold for four times what I'd paid for them. I was able to pay off the balance on the commercial lots in just four months. I had the foundations of a new business in South Africa if we needed to leave Rhodesia.

After completing that purchase in Phalaborwa, Anne and I decided to visit her family in South Africa every three months, bringing in some extra traveler's cheques each time to increase our savings account. We wanted to build a nest egg to build the mall. Since the border was just a few hours away from Fort Victoria, and she had a large extended family in South Africa, we took short trips there whenever possible.

We were incredibly proud when the Coronet was voted the best-looking drive-in cinema in Rhodesia! Later, we were listed as one of the top five drive-ins in the region of southern Africa. Our hard work and planning were paying off! We felt so confident we decided to add another business to our portfolio, a commercial laundry plant and dry-cleaning business.

For such a large city, Fort Victoria had only one commercial laundry to serve all the hotels and hospitals. Some people were not happy with their work or pricing. I sensed an opportunity.

"Bill, how are you doing? This is Nick Haritatos."

"Hey Nick, we miss you here in Gatooma, my friend! I read about your drive-in in the newspaper. It looks amazing. What can I do for you?"

"Bill, I want to learn about the laundry business. May I come over and visit your operation?"

When I toured Bill's large laundry business, I noticed it depended on large machines and streamlined processes, just like a bakery. A laundry business would not be hard for me to manage and if I had seasoned employees, it wouldn't take too much of my time away from the drive-in.

Bill told me he knew a man in Gatooma who wanted to sell his commercial laundry business and get out of Rhodesia. "Nick, why don't I help you buy that business?" Bill suggested. "You could move all the equipment over to Fort Victoria by truck. It would be easier and cheaper to buy used equipment, so all you'd need is a location. Heck, I bet the employees might even move, too, if you offered them a good deal."

"Why would you help me do that, Bill?"

"First, because you are my friend and I'm a good guy. Second, you'd be eliminating my biggest competitor in Gatooma!" Bill chuckled.

I went home and talked with Anne, who agreed this would be a wise investment. I made quite a few trips over to Gatooma negotiating the deal and learning about operations from Bill. After purchasing the business, I met with the staff and invited all of them to move to Fort Victoria, offering a bonus and help finding new housing for their families. Thankfully, they all agreed to follow the business to its new location, so I would have a well-trained and experienced staff immediately.

Moving the laundry was a large process with many moving pieces, but I enjoyed the challenge. It was fun for me to devise ways to set up the plant as efficiently as possible.

Anne kept operations running smoothly at the Coronet while I devoted many hours into moving the laundry and giving it a competitive advantage. We set up a sixty-minute express service, a customer loyalty rewards program, and other initiatives to foster high quality and outstanding customer service.

Within a year of our grand opening, we were the largest laundry business in Fort Victoria. We did commercial laundry for many hotels, hospitals, and restaurants. Plus, we had kiosks in several neighborhoods for consumer dry-cleaning and laundry. We concentrated all our services on the large plant, using a fleet of vans to move laundry to our commercial customers and neighborhood kiosks. Planning the logistics for this business was a challenge, but I enjoyed finding ways to solve it.

I felt proud when Anne's father approached me as a potential investor in his new gold mine. I was also a little wary. My father-in-law was a mining engineer and explosives expert employed as the chief mining inspector for the government. He certainly knew about mining; however, I wasn't sure about his business acumen as he'd been a government employee for most of his life.

He wanted to buy an abandoned mine called Step-Lively, which had been closed after a terrible accident where several people died. He was a hot-tempered man who'd never seemed particularly fond of me, so I expected he would not want to involve me in daily operations.

I struggled with this decision until Anne's mother came to visit. She was very persuasive. I'd always liked her and was grateful she encouraged Anne to marry me, so it felt as if I owed her a favor. How could I deny my darling wife and her mother?

Investing in a family business was second nature to me, so eventually I became a passive investor in the Step-Lively mine.

It did feel as if our lives were golden. Anne and I had a great life in Fort Victoria, filled with good friends, two profitable businesses, and a sterling reputation in the community. Yet, every time I opened a newspaper or watched the news, I saw more stories about atrocities and guerilla activities in northern Rhodesia. Most of the people I knew, including Peter and Cathreen, believed the Rhodesian military was so strong the guerillas would eventually give up and go away. My gut told me differently. Danger was lurking just over the horizon.

Chapter 10: Tarnished Dreams

"I know that guy!" I exclaimed to Anne one morning while I was reading the newspaper at the breakfast table. "Look, that man, Robert Mugabe, I used to give him rides in the bakery van."

"Nick, he's a terrorist, the leader of one of the fiercest guerilla factions trying to topple the government. Do you really know him?" Anne was incredulous. Her eyes grew wide as I told her about driving the bakery van deep in Shona territory about eighty miles outside of Gatooma when I was a teen. "What was Mugabe like?" she asked.

"He was nice to me. I remember he was very smart and spoke English perfectly. He told me he was a teacher and I believed him. He spoke in that way teachers do, measured and logical. I can't believe Robert Mugabe is now a wanted man!"

As we read the newspaper article, my sense of shock deepened. Mugabe was the leader of a terrorist group actively working to overthrow the Rhodesian government. The attacks started several years earlier and had grown in intensity and violence. Now, in 1974, we read and heard stories every day about terrible atrocities including kidnappings, murders, burning of farms, and even mutilation of people who resisted.

A wave of revolution was sweeping through central and southern Africa. Mozambique, on Rhodesia's eastern border, fell to Marxists, as had Zambia on the northern border.

My father was right: things in Rhodesia were becoming dangerous. Anne and I decided to wait on building our new house at the Coronet for a while because of the unrest.

A few months later, I received a registered letter from the Ministries of Defense and of Internal Affairs informing me I was drafted into a special program of civilian administration under the Department of Internal Affairs working in conjunction with the military.

I couldn't believe it! I was a businessman, not a soldier. In fact, I hated war and remembered the scars it left on my father.

The letter went on to detail the position I'd have. The government was creating a series of protected villages, walled enclosures to protect up to five thousand citizens who would be moved from tribal lands in dangerous border areas. Businessmen like me were being drafted to serve as Village Commanders, a position that straddled city administration and military reconnaissance in the jungle areas surrounding the villages.

I was angry and frustrated, so I made an appointment with the Provincial Commissioner for Internal Affairs and his team in Fort Victoria. Both the Commissioner and his two aides were regular customers of the Coronet, so I hoped to find a way to decline the position.

"Commissioner, you know me. I'm busy taking care of the citizens of Fort Victoria, at the drive-in and the laundry and dry cleaning business. You know I'm providing good jobs and bringing tourists to the city. I simply can't afford to leave my businesses for long periods of time. I'd like to respectfully decline the invitation to be a Village Commander."

"Mr. Haritatos, you are one of Rhodesia's finest businessmen. It's well known you speak Shona and Fanakalo flawlessly. The country needs men like you. Our President is counting on your help, which is an honor. You should be proud to serve." The Commissioner said, "I can help you a little. I'll ensure you are sent only to the best villages, ones near here where there is no danger. It won't be too hard. You are a talented man. You can do this easily."

His flattery did not convince me. "Sir, with all due respect, I cannot do this. I have a young wife who would be left alone to run my businesses. I don't have any family here to help her. I believe in peace. I don't want to be part of any military action."

"Mr. Haritatos," the Commissioner said sternly, "you do not understand the situation. Let me be very clear. You are drafted into this position, by order of the Rhodesian government. There is nothing you can do except obey. If you fail to report for your training as instructed, you will face arrest, be court-martialed, and jailed."

Defeated, I went home and told Anne the bad news. We had just six weeks before I had to report for training. Anne and I began to make plans.

Because I'd spent so much time creating processes and training the staff, I was confident our loyal managers would help Anne to keep the laundry and drive-in operating smoothly, but Anne would have to take care of all the finances and oversee operations at both locations. I hated to leave her alone with such a significant burden, but she was brave and willing to do everything possible to protect herself and our businesses.

Even though neither of us liked guns, I bought her a pistol and taught her how to shoot it, as well as my double barrel shotgun. I never dreamed I'd have to show my gentle wife how to shoot guns, but it was important she could defend herself. This was a nightmare for both of us.

The time flew by, and all too soon I began my four-month training in Salisbury. Every Monday morning I'd kiss Anne goodbye at 4 a.m. and drive to the capital city. Thankfully, I was permitted to return home each weekend, but the separation was difficult for both of us, especially since we could not write or call each other at all. Every night I longed to talk with Anne, to hear her sweet voice and wise counsel. I also worried about how she was handling two businesses by herself.

The rigorous training combined administrative tasks with military expertise. My training group included other businessmen and owners of large farms from across the country, brought together in this new government initiative. I was the youngest participant in the program.

We learned how to shoot a variety of guns, bush fighting techniques and combat, tracking, radio communications, how to interface with the military, emergency protocols, and a wide variety of procedures, reporting, and administrative duties.

It seemed incredible I was learning how to shoot a machine gun and how to interrogate a prisoner to determine if he were a rebel spy. I even learned how to evade capture and how to survive under torture if I was captured.

I'd always cherished my freedom and autonomy. Now, my time and my future rested in the hands of a government agency. I felt as if I was trapped in a war movie at the Coronet, but this situation was very real.

Four months later, my uniform had three stars on it and a pin that read Commander. Supposedly, I was well-prepared to shoulder responsibility for the safety of up to five thousand civilians, as well as a group of up to forty armed guards. I wasn't even thirty years old and had no idea how I'd cope with these monumental demands.

I'd had tearful goodbyes with Anne, my parents, and siblings. My stomach clenched as soon as I arrived at the base in Salisbury. When I saw the transport vehicle, I realized the seriousness of my mission. Heavy armor plating surrounded the truck. The bottom of the vehicle was designed like the bottom of a boat, complete with a heavy metal floor and sandbags in case the truck drove over a landmine on our journey to the villages. There were slots in the armor-plated metal walls for rifles.

As I entered the transport for my journey north, I realized I'd need all my courage, intelligence, and determination to survive the next six weeks and make the journey back home to Anne.

I felt like a different person, unfamiliar to myself.

As I'd been trained, I'd stopped shaving a few weeks before my deployment and had a scruffy black beard, which would provide camouflage in the jungle. I would not shave again until I returned home.

No longer the well-groomed professional man who had a smile for everyone and a real desire to delight customers, I steeled myself to be suspicious, watchful, and alert at every moment. I was entering a war zone and had to conduct myself properly or I'd be killed.

When we arrived at the protected village, I saw the large fence enclosing about a thousand traditional homes, made of cut trees and mud with thatched roofs. Each village was built in a remote area, constructed in the same strategic manner, with about one thousand yards of cleared area between the fence and the thick jungle vegetation.

Home to three thousand African villagers from the surrounding areas, there was just one gate into the village, manned by guards with rifles. People could leave the village during daylight hours to tend their farms. After dark, the gates were locked, and anyone found lurking outside the fence or in the area near the entrance gate would be shot because it was a no-go operational area.

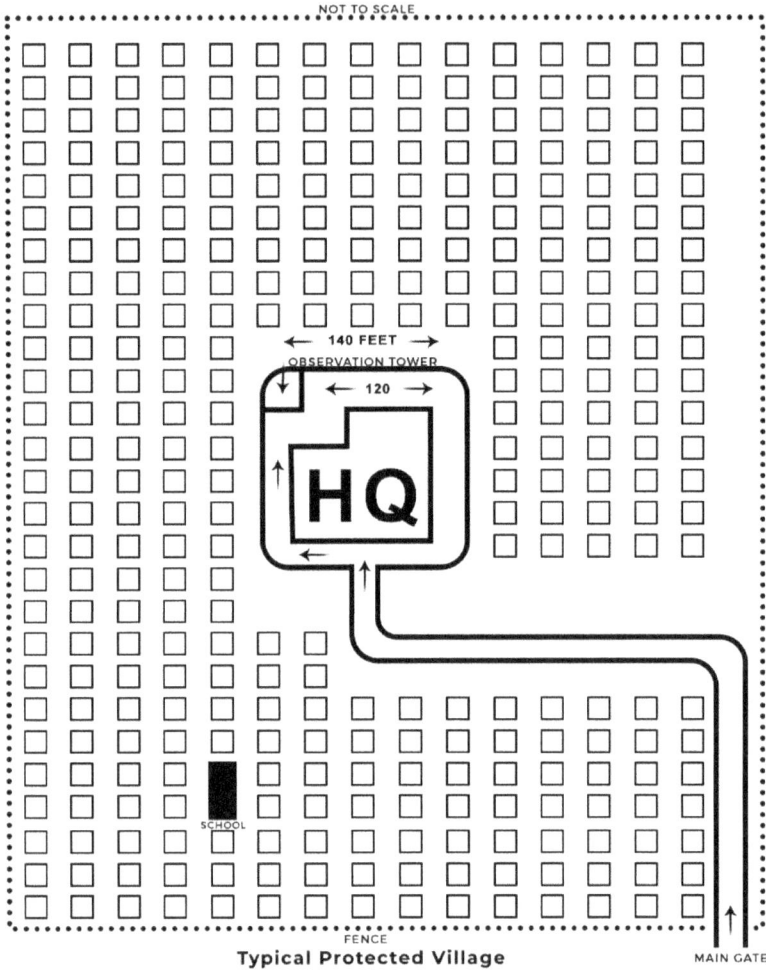

Typical Protected Village

The road leading from the entrance curved through row after row of mud huts which were built close together. No one was allowed to drive inside the village except for command staff or military vehicles. The winding entrance roads delayed attackers from storming the gates and quickly reaching the command center. Along with the civilian housing, the villages had a school and a community building.

The administrative compound lay in the center of the village in an excavated area surrounded by earthen walls seven feet thick and eight feet tall. All the buildings in the command center were sunken into the ground so the roof was lower than the earthen walls, designed to protect the area from mortar bombs, rocket propelled grenades, shoulder fired missiles, and machine gun fire for at least eight to ten hours. A thirty-five-foot guard tower in this area provided oversight of the entire village and the area far beyond the fences. This tower had an observation deck with machine guns facing in all directions, radio antennae, and a two-foot mound of sandbags around the bottom for stabilization. If a vehicle or suicide team smashed through the entrance gate or mortar bombs flew into the compound, the soldiers in the guard tower were ready to open fire with their machine guns.

I was now in charge of this huge village, just me and a deputy commander, the only Caucasians in the village. Our village was supported by a small group of soldiers and a group of about thirty armed guards, a tiny force to protect thousands of lives from an unknown number of guerillas intent on malice. Spies and informants lurked in each village, indistinguishable from the other villagers, passing information to the terrorists and trying to convince others to join their cause. I had no idea how I would endure the next six weeks.

After my briefing with the departing Commander, I had to strap on a machine gun and place belts with 100 rounds of ammunition around my shoulders. I was required to have that gun on my body during all waking hours and keep it beside my bed at night.

Then, I set about meeting all the guards and military personnel, visiting the tower and front gate as well as touring the village. It was important for me to establish my authority by meeting each member of the military and guard staff. I had to rely on their knowledge of the village and surrounding area. I'd ask each man about his duties, if he had enough supplies, and if there were any changes he felt needed to be made.

I believed it was important to communicate I was there for a purpose, not a holiday. I used my business skills to quickly earn respect and cooperation by listening, building teamwork, and ensuring my team knew I was there to support them. These men would walk behind me during dangerous patrols so I wanted them to know I would protect them, trusting they would protect me in turn.

Next, I arranged for a formal meeting with the village chief. During our meeting, the chief seemed surprised I could communicate with him easily in Shona. I treated him with great respect and asked many questions about the village, especially if there were anything the villagers needed. At the end of the meeting, I told him it was my intention to work together with him for the good of the village. He seemed to like that message.

As I settled into life in the village, my days followed a predictable pattern. I began at dawn with a briefing to discuss intelligence from our confidential sources. Each village had trusted informants providing daily reports of events inside the village and in the nearby area. While the protected villages were isolated, we were in constant communication with the government and military. I'd also review daily intelligence reports from the military command and government, including the location of any military maneuvers in the area. Based on the information in the intelligence reports, I'd decide when and where to patrol in the areas outside of the fence, looking for terrorists as was required.

Each day we would patrol on foot for three to five hours. The jungle was full of guerillas hiding and watching the village, so it was vital we varied both the routes and hours of the patrols. It was my responsibility to plan, coordinate, and lead the patrols, leaving my deputy commander behind in the command center where he would plot our location on a large operations map of the area there. I'd radio him every five to ten minutes to update him on our most current positions.

The stakes were high. The guerillas moved at night and by daybreak were hiding in the jungle, bush, or near large boulders, prepared for ambush. Armed with rocket propelled grenades (RPGs) and AK 47 rifles, when they opened fire on our patrols, it was dangerous and deadly. We had to be prepared to spot land mines, booby traps, and defend ourselves from surprise attacks.

Before leaving, I would blacken all my exposed skin with a special cream so I would blend into the bush. As commander, I walked in the front of the line, keeping my eyes peeled for danger, as well as making eye contact with my men. It would have been easy for a spy to infiltrate the guards and shoot me in the back at any moment.

We were deep in the bush in primitive areas with heavy vegetation and no roads. The bush was untamed and hostile. In the hot, humid wilderness, we might encounter packs of dangerous large animals like baboons, elephants, or water buffalo. There were fire ants, snakes, ticks, and poisonous insects. The air was full of the sounds of the jungle and thousands of birds, often masking the quiet tread of footsteps. I even had to pay attention to the wind to ensure no one downwind would catch our scent and attack.

My senses were on high alert for any signs of danger. I smelled smoke from fires or cigarettes, even catching the scent of a human. My ears were attuned to the slightest sound, which might mean a group of guerillas were hiding and preparing to open fire. I also used my training in tracking to examine footprints in the soil and determine when they'd walked there.

There was valuable information to be gathered from footwear. I scrutinized the boots and shoes people wore, getting information about gender and size, and who supplied the shoes. I saw boots and shoes made in China, North Korea, Cuba, and the Soviet Union. We deduced that if guerillas were wearing shoes from a particular nation, they would have weaponry and training from that nation. But tracking was complicated. It frequently rained, distorting prints, and the terrorists knew to walk in rivers and on rocks, make turns, and even walk backward to disguise their tracks.

They also had underground bases deep in the jungle. These small bases were heavily camouflaged by vegetation, allowing the guerillas to attack patrols from behind if we walked by them unaware. I had to use everything I had to protect myself and my people each day of my deployment, but the patrols were the most dangerous part.

The terrorists were heavily armed and well-trained in guerilla tactics so each encounter might quickly become a life-or-death situation for my patrol. When we discovered groups of terrorists, they would wait until we came close, then open fire or scatter in every direction. Because the guerillas had their camps across our borders, they would do anything possible to return to base, including swimming across lakes and rivers, hiding in the jungle, or setting traps to deter us as we chased them in hot pursuit.

Officially, our job was surveillance and reporting to the military, who would come to the area with soldiers, helicopters manned with machine guns, and other equipment to engage and capture the insurgents. We civilians were to cause disruption and continue surveillance until the military arrived. It was extremely dangerous, and I was responsible for everyone's safety.

"Down, now!" I'd whisper to my patrol whenever I sensed someone nearby. Seconds later bullets would be flying, and we'd be in the middle of an ambush. Soon our civilian 'disruption and surveillance' turned into a gunfight and mad chase through the jungle trying to prevent our enemies from killing us or escaping.

When we discovered someone in the jungle, he was most likely a terrorist. No ordinary citizens walked there. We would shout and come up with our guns drawn, ordering the person or group to lie on the ground, watching carefully for others hidden in the trees, behind rocks waiting to attack us. If there was any threat to our safety, I had to immediately give the order to open fire.

It was them or us. There was no time to doubt my instincts. Hesitation would cost the lives of my patrol and perhaps my own.

In time, I quickly learned how to spot guerillas as I interrogated them in the bush. They were always very thin and wore extremely dirty clothing from weeks of hiding in the jungle. They would have marks on their shoulders and backs from rifle belts. If they had boots on, they were most likely terrorists. The tread of their boots often told me everything I needed to know. If I felt certain they were guerillas, I would turn them over to the military for interrogation.

In the rare occasions where I was unsure, we would bring a prisoner back to the village for further interrogation.

My people were horribly injured on some of our patrols, wounded by gun fire or landmines. Landmines were often buried under the soil, tripped by fishing wire strung between trees, or by being stepped on. These injuries occurred suddenly and with devastating force.

We carried first aid supplies on each patrol. I always prayed I would not have to use them. When I lost men from my patrol, I felt as if I'd failed in my mission to protect them.

Over time, I had to learn to steel myself to the danger and the blood. I wondered what I was doing in the middle of a bush war. I was a businessman who believed in treating people with respect and kindness. It seemed like I was living on another planet where my life was at risk every moment. I never relaxed for a moment during the entire six weeks.

When I was not on patrol, I addressed administrative duties within the village. There were always problems to solve and safety measures to supervise. I would vary my activities, unexpectedly visiting the guard towers at random times during the day or night, meet with my deputies, and walk around the village.

I rarely slept for more than five or six hours each night. There was too much to do. I was always on the alert, ready to grab my machine gun at any moment.

One evening right before dinner, I heard bombs approaching the village and ran to the control room. Large mortars with up to fifteen pounds of explosives started to hit the ground, followed by rocket propelled grenades. Machine gun fire came after that.

All the villagers ran to their houses and hid under their beds. The guards sprang into action and went to their designated locations. We always drilled for attacks, and everyone knew what to do.

The men in the tower started returning fire in the direction of the attack and we radioed the military base. We had enough ammunition to defend the village for ten hours. The next thirty minutes of bombing felt like an eternity in Hell. Thankfully, we were able to repel the attack.

It was a terrible burden to carry one hundred rounds of ammunition and a machine gun on my body every day. The emotional burden was even greater. I knew many of the young men attacking us had been kidnapped, brainwashed, and seduced by false promises of wealth without work. I understood their culture and that they wanted a good life, like I did. However, they were seeking that good life through violence.

When my six-week deployment ended, I climbed back in an armored vehicle for the long ride back to Salisbury. I was a different person than when I'd arrived—horrified by the cruelty of war, scarred by the bloodshed, and exhausted physically and emotionally. The worse of it was the knowledge I'd be in a new village, facing the same danger, in just six weeks' time.

Chapter 11: Winning Hearts and Minds

Each time I had to return to the protected villages, it was more difficult. The days at the villages passed in unrelenting loneliness and stress. I had no contact with Anne or anyone outside the village except for nearby military officers.

It was difficult to go to a new village every deployment without any relationships. There was no way to know who to trust or who might be a spy or informant. I could only rely on my wits, my faith, my machine gun, and my courage.

The bush war intensified and spread further into Rhodesia. One of my neighbors from Fort Victoria, another Village Commander, was killed on patrol. Other commanders encountered landmines and suffered horrific injuries. A few committed suicide. Many of the men I trained with left Rhodesia because of the terrible risk to their safety, especially if they had children. It was as if we were financial prisoners, unable to leave Rhodesia because of our businesses.

At the time, no one knew about Post Traumatic Stress and the toll combat exacted. I never wanted to be a soldier, yet at least half of my time was spent with a gun in my hands. It seemed as if the government sent me and the others to war as a small cog in a large machine. If any of us became damaged, we were tossed away and replaced.

I was careful not to tell Anne about the dangerous aspects of my work, but she noticed a change in me before I had to report for duty. I always felt deep sadness wash over me. I grew quiet and began to have terrible nightmares.

Prior to each new deployment, I would do everything possible to arrange things at the drive-in and laundry to make it easy on Anne while I was away. I'd inform my family, who lived two hundred miles away so they could check on Anne while I was gone. Sometimes one of Anne's sisters would come to stay with her while I was away.

On the day of each new deployment, Anne and I would leave our house at 4 a.m. and drive 190 miles to the armory in Salisbury to get my next assignment and equipment.

It felt like torture each time I kissed her goodbye, knowing I'd have no way to talk with her, protect her, or help her for the next six weeks.

Anne was brave and rarely complained, working hard to keep my spirits up, but months and months of stress was taking a toll on each of us.

Yet, with each deployment, I was determined to care for the people of my village. My language skills were invaluable. I was often the only person in command able to speak the local languages. Thanks to my time in the bakery and out on the delivery routes and my business customers of different cultures, I could communicate with everyone. I also understood and respected their culture.

It was a huge undertaking to be responsible for the safety of thousands of people—everyone in the village and my guards and military personnel. I had to be very diplomatic, earn respect, and help the people believe I was there to protect them from the terrorists.

I realized it was imperative to win the hearts and minds of the people.

We were in a guerilla war. There were spies in every camp, competing with us to turn villages to their cause. Even though the villages seemed friendly, there was no way to determine friend from foe. I could never fully trust anyone.

Still, I required my staff to treat each person with the utmost respect. Like my father taught me in the bakery, I realized the importance of gaining loyalty by serving each person to the best of my ability.

Whenever I came to a village, I set up a meeting with the chief right away. I would talk about how I was there to help and protect the people and hear any concerns. Because I spoke their language, they were more willing to trust me. Some chiefs would send food to my quarters as a sign of trust and respect, even though food was precious.

Because I wanted to win loyalty for our cause and for me personally, I decided to try some new ideas. One day I noticed some children trying to play soccer with a ball they made from crumpled up paper and tape. African people love soccer; it unites everyone.

I decided to ask about starting soccer games in the villages, first getting permission from the military Colonel and Internal Affairs Civilian Headquarters. They thought it was a brilliant idea and moved quickly to supply funds for tools, goal posts, and soccer balls.

Next, I called a meeting with the Chief, the fathers, and youngsters, proposing we work together to build a soccer field in the village for the children. I told the men we would supply the wheelbarrows, shovels, and equipment for the field. I would put the soccer field just outside the fence but close to the front entrance where the guards could monitor the children's safety while they played. The fathers would build the field, set up the teams and serve as coaches. The soccer projects were all successful. They built goodwill and gave the children many hours of enjoyment.

I also requested more teachers. Each village had a school but needed more support to teach the children to read and write. I asked the village chiefs if they would like to improve the schools and suggested adding classes in English so the children might have more job opportunities.

The leaders were happy about this. Every chief was supportive of efforts to help the children with better schooling and soccer teams.

In time, the chiefs grew to like me and appreciated my efforts. Often, when it was nearing the end of my six-week stay, the chief would visit me and ask me to stay on. I replied I had to return to care for my wife and my business, which they understood. It felt good to know I was making a difference and helping people, even during a dangerous and terrible time.

I did not like to interrogate anyone inside the village, but sometimes I had no choice when we captured a suspected terrorist on patrol. This was dangerous because I knew it might break the bonds of goodwill I was building with the villagers. Also, it put us at a greater risk for attacks from the comrades of the captured men. Our community was not a military base. The military bases were located fifty to seventy-five miles south of the protected villages. Military personnel came and went while we stayed on the front lines.

At that time, the military also hired men who had retired from battles in South Africa, Australia, the United States, United Kingdom, France, and other countries as contract soldiers. They were good soldiers, aggressive, and hardcore military men. However, they did not know local customs, culture, and beliefs. Many were quick to pull a trigger. They also had no ties to a village or any of the local people. They would do the interrogations and then take off, leaving me to deal with any consequences and rebuild trust.

So, I instituted a new policy. Whenever captured guerillas arrived in the village, I instructed my deputies to notify the military officer to speak to me directly before beginning an interrogation.

When we had a prisoner who appeared to be a hard-core guerilla, I asked the military to take him to their base for serious interrogation. I would suggest they leave the younger men with me and return to their patrols, returning in a few days. I would have answers for them when they returned.

Many of the military commanders doubted I would be able to deliver any useful information. However, since I oversaw the village, they reluctantly agreed. Other village commanders did not engage in interrogations, but I felt I might be able to help some of the younger men with a different approach.

In the interrogation room, I would talk with just one person at a time and always speak in their language, which was very surprising to them. It was easy for me to spot men who were guerillas. They had marks on their bodies from carrying rifles, machine guns, and ammunition. They had hard calluses and scars, especially on their shoulders. Their feet were blistered and cracked from walking many miles. Most were thin, starved, and malnourished.

I had my deputy with me taking notes and taping everything on a recorder. I would approach the young man very kindly, saying he would not be hurt. My goal was to make him remember his humanity, breaking through his hard shell. I would speak softly and slowly, telling the young man I understood he was kidnapped, brainwashed, or forced to fight with the rebels. I'd remind him how he was letting his family down and hurting his own people. Then, I'd talk about how he had not received any money, just been given empty promises.

Most of the time, these young men would break down in tears. They were young, uneducated kids who took a wrong turn or were seduced by promises from communists—indoctrinated by them. I believed some could be helped. They were more likely to give vital information to someone kind instead of a person using threats or violence.

Next, I would try to make him laugh a bit and see some hope for a better future. Depending on what he told me and how much he cooperated with me, I might help him escape from those who were forcing him to kill and harm others. I'd offer comfort, look them in the eyes, touch their shoulder, and tell them it was safe to speak with me.

Most would begin to tell me everything they knew: how they were recruited, the routes used to cross the border, the location of their training camps, and a variety of information about communications, weapons, people who hid or supplied them, and their tactics.

These interrogations will live in my memory for the rest of my life. I did not enjoy them, but I felt they were a service to humanity. Through my efforts, I extracted important information without violence. I knew I could not stay in a village where men were subjected to torture or even put to death. It was better to handle the interrogations myself, so they were humane.

To my knowledge, I was the only village commander to conduct interrogations.

I understood broken promises too. By 1976, I'd been serving as a Village Commander for two years and felt disheartened and discouraged. When I was drafted, I was promised deployments to villages near Fort Victoria. Instead, I was continually sent to the farthest borders in the most dangerous areas.

Even though I asked for closer deployments, my requests went unheeded. My six-week deployments were sometimes extended to twelve weeks with little to no warning.

Worst of all, from my interrogations I learned the guerillas were gaining in strength and foreign support. There were more battles, attacks, and acts of terror on all the northern and eastern borders.

Many Rhodesians began to emigrate and move their assets out of the country. I remembered seeing that long line of cars full of frightened people from the Belgian Congo driving to safety years earlier. I constantly wondered if it was time for Anne and me to flee towards safety.

Chapter 12: Family Comes First

"Sweetie, I want to have a baby," Anne said when I'd been home for a few days. "If you are killed, I want to have part of you with me. I just can't stop thinking about those plane crashes."

As I watched my wife with tears in her eyes, my heart broke. Every time I had to leave Anne, I wondered if I would even survive the trip to the village, let alone six weeks in a war zone. But I was more worried about her safety.

When she was in Fort Victoria, she was relatively safe. However, there were a few occasions when the films for the drive-in were not delivered on time, and she had to drive 380 miles round trip to fetch them from the capital city.

Of course, Anne was smart; she took her guns and one of our employees with her, but it was still a perilous journey in a country in the middle of an undeclared war.

Recently, two civilian airline planes had been shot down by Russian-supplied surface-to-air missiles. The guerillas were being supported by Russia, North Korea, China, Cuba, and the Eastern Bloc. The bush war was escalating into central Rhodesia and becoming more violent. The newspapers and television news reports were full of reports of terrible atrocities.

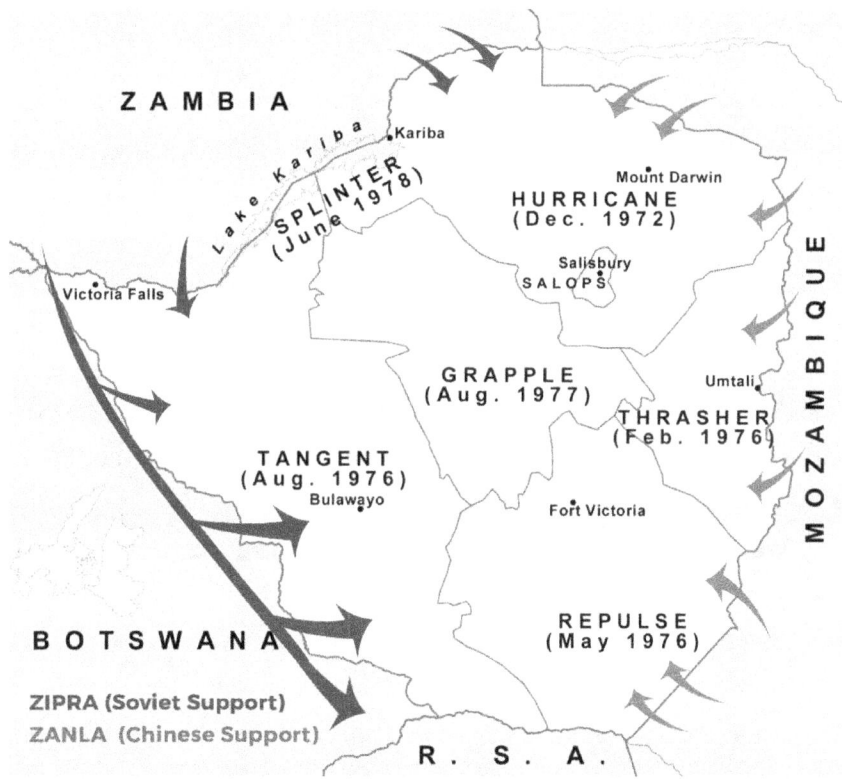

Operational areas of the Rhodesian Security Forces during the Bush War in the 1970s (arrows and notation in bottom left corner added): Cilliers, Jakkie. *Counter-Insurgency in Rhodesia.* London: Sydney & Dover, December 1984. New Hampshire: Croom Helm, 29.

No wonder Anne feared for my life. I did, as well.

Beyond all that worry, every day I agonized over the future of my businesses and the life we had built in Fort Victoria. Everything we'd worked so hard for was at risk. How could I bring a child into this dangerous situation?

After another long, harrowing journey home from a deployment, I went to my command center. There was a new provincial commissioner there who was very rude. Once again, I asked if my next assignment might be to a village within half a day of Fort Victoria, explaining how much more efficient it would be and how vital my time was to manage all the responsibilities of my businesses.

He angrily replied, "You can close those businesses! They are not important. You will go where we send you, whenever we tell you to go."

I lost my temper. I got up from my chair and walked around the table to where he sat and said, "You don't know anything. You are just an employee of the government who doesn't even own a home. I built everything I have with my own hands. I provide many people with work and important things. Business provides the money to run our country. Without men like me, you'd have no money for this war. You will have nothing."

We continued to argue. Finally, I told him I was done, and I'd be leaving the country.

He said, "I don't care what you say. You have a responsibility to Rhodesia and will fulfill it. You have no choice."

Anne and I decided it was time to go to South Africa and began quietly making plans. Thankfully, we'd planned and knew we could stay with Auntie Poppie and Uncle Willem.

As a citizen of South Africa, Anne would have no trouble crossing the border. We knew it might be challenging for me to leave the country. Although I was entitled to residency in South Africa because I was married to a citizen, the Rhodesian government had a private agreement with South Africa to delay the immigration process for young professional men like me, especially one serving the government.

"Peter, it's time for you to think about leaving Rhodesia. In fact, all of you should go. Baba, you were right, things are getting too dangerous here for us." I said as we all gathered around Mama's table.

"I can't leave my businesses, Nick. I'd lose everything. I'm just not brave like you. I'm staying here." Peter hadn't been drafted into the Village Commander program. He was drafted as a diesel truck mechanic and stayed in the capital. He had not seen any combat. He wasn't willing to leave his many businesses and huge ranch.

I listened with sorrow as Cathreen and my parents all found reasons why they were not willing to change their lives and leave Rhodesia either. My family felt safe because they only knew what they read in the newspapers and in the media. They had no idea what I'd seen in the villages and the disturbing reports of the increasing tide of guerilla activity. I tried to inform them without scaring them, but they did not believe me.

By the end of the evening, they knew Anne and I were planning to leave at some point, but we kept the details vague to protect them. The less they knew, the better.

Baba took me aside as we were leaving, "My son, I know there is much you cannot say. You are right to leave. Go soon before you are killed. Your mother and I are old. We will be alright. I give you my blessings and prayers. Have courage and build a new life in a place you can thrive."

Those words from my father gave me strength and courage. It would be dangerous to leave Rhodesia. I had no idea if I would be arrested and thrown into jail. However, remaining in the Village Commander position was a death sentence. I'd most likely be killed and my businesses would die from neglect. If I were going to become a father, I had to think more about protecting my family instead of sacrificing for a government who cared little for me.

Anne and I decided we'd leave as soon as possible. She started working on all the arrangements. I was immensely grateful I had such a wise and intelligent wife who was a true partner to me in every aspect of my life.

One of the most formidable obstacles we faced was applying to take our own money out of the country. We were only allowed to take $900 out of the county via official channels. However, I had already moved most of my savings out of the country on our many visits to South Africa. We were so thankful we'd planned for this emergency and had cash and some commercial property in South Africa. It wasn't as much as I would have liked, but we would be able to survive for some time.

Before we knew it, my next deployment arrived. Once again, I left my wife and my home for six weeks of stress, danger, and crushing responsibility in a new protected village. After six weeks, I was packed and ready to go home. However, when the transport truck arrived, the driver gave me a letter that said I had to stay for another six weeks.

It was incredibly frustrating. Anne would be waiting in Salisbury to pick me up and I had no way to reach her. This was clearly a retaliation from the new provincial commissioner I argued with, the one who disrespected me and my business responsibilities. This was the final straw.

"Deputy, you are now in command of this village." I notified my shocked assistant, then said to the driver. "Let's go, I'm needed urgently in Salisbury." No one had any idea what I'd read in that letter, so I gambled on my authority to get me in that truck and away from the village before anyone realized what was happening. I jumped in the truck, and as I endured the long ride, I wondered if I would be jailed as a deserter when I arrived at the base.

When I arrived at the base in Salisbury, I was braced for arrest or conflict. Instead of just leaving my gun and ammunition as usual, I told the clerks I wanted to turn in all my equipment.

"I am resigning from my position as a Village Commander effective immediately."

"Sir, we cannot accept your resignation. Keep your equipment. You'll need it for your next deployment."

"You are not listening. I am resigning whether you like it or not."

Finally, I put everything in a pile on a table—my machine gun, ammunition, boots, full uniform, even the hat I wore. I turned smartly and walked out of the office.

"Anne, sweetie, let's get out of here right now. I just quit."

I jumped behind the wheel of Anne's red Jag and hit the gas. We drove quickly out of the lot and held hands until we got out of Salisbury.

"Nick, I thought they were going to chase us down. I felt like we were Bonnie and Clyde!" Anne was laughing and crying at the same time. Finally, she took a deep breath and said, "I have some news. I'm pregnant."

I pulled the car off the highway and took my beloved wife in my arms. My heart was so full of joy I wept.

Within six weeks, we were on the highway to South Africa. Anne was able to arrange for a moving van to take our possessions to a storage center in Durban using her South African passport. We rented our beautiful Coronet Drive-In Cinema to a friend at an exceptionally low rent and sold the laundry at a fire sale price. I also walked away from my investment in my father-in-law's gold mine, telling him if he lost it, he did not need to reimburse me.

Anne's father was terribly angry. He'd been born in Rhodesia and was stubbornly clinging to the idea the government would survive, ignoring all the evidence to the contrary. He called me a coward and many other hurtful things. The one that stung the most was that I was taking the easy way out.

My years of service in the protected villages were not easy. I put my life on the line for Rhodesia every day during my deployments. I had no choice but to walk away from that argument and focus on my family.

It was heartbreaking for Anne and me to endure such substantial financial and emotional losses after we'd worked so hard. In all, we were walking away from at least five million dollars. However, the importance of money paled in comparison to the safety and wellbeing of my Anne and our child. We knew we were able to start over and find a way to build a new life together, which was most important of all.

Finally, the day arrived for us to leave. We both had tears in our eyes as we drove away from the Coronet, our beautiful business born out of our vision and passion. We'd been so happy there and worked so hard to build success. It was a bittersweet moment. As we drove towards the border in Anne's red Jaguar, we hoped we could cross without any problems. I was waiting to be arrested at any moment in the last six weeks, waiting for the police or military to show up at my door and take me into custody.

I had my Greek passport in hand, along with Anne's South African one. When we got to the border, the guards started to question us. Anne said firmly, "I am a pregnant citizen of South Africa, and I'm taking my husband home with me."

The guards, moved by her words, let us through.

A huge weight lifted off my shoulders as soon as we crossed the border. I focused on the potential waiting for me in South Africa. It was time to put all my war experiences in a box, shut it tightly, and envision a better future.

As the red Jaguar took us deeper into South Africa, the more excited I became. I would make a beautiful life there. There were many opportunities in front of me. Anne was beside me. I resolved to not allow the scars of the past to hinder me and walk into the future with courage and enthusiasm.

Chapter 13: Fortune's Smile

———————————————➤

"You're here! Welcome to your new home!" Uncle Willem exclaimed as Anne and I drove up his driveway. The trip from the border to Phalaborwa went quickly because we were so thrilled to be safely away from Rhodesia and eager to begin our new lives. By then, I'd owned businesses for fifteen years and was confident I would become successful in South Africa, the wealthiest nation on the African continent, and one of the wealthiest in the world at the time.

As always, Uncle Willem and Auntie Poppie treated us just like their own children, insisting we stay with them instead of renting an apartment. Our first goal was to sort out my residency status. Just a few months prior to leaving Rhodesia, I'd visited the South African embassy in Salisbury to apply for residency.

"I'm sorry Mr. Haritatos, I cannot grant you residency at this time," the official sneered after barely glancing at my application.

"May I ask why not?" As I'd been warned, the agreement with South Africa was becoming a reality, to deny men residency, especially men like me who were commanders of the protected villages or members of the military. However, some of my friends had been blocked from entering since they were not married to a South African citizen.

"We are not processing any applications today. Come back another time."

I didn't believe the immigration officer but decided to wait until I was out of Rhodesia to try again. We mentioned our challenge to Uncle Willem.

"Not to worry, Nick! One of my friends at the hospital is always bragging about how he knows the Minister of Energy who is also the MP of this area. I'll ask my friend to set up a meeting for you."

A few days later, we drove to the Minister's home. He listened to our story and then assured us Anne's citizenship guaranteed my residency status.

"You've been through so much and should not have been given any problems at our embassy. Let me contact the Secretary of Immigration personally and secure an appointment for you."

Thanks to Uncle Willem, I felt much better my paperwork would be approved.

A few weeks later, we were invited to meet with the Secretary of Immigration in Pretoria, a seven-hour drive. We gathered all our documentation and arrived at the office dressed in our most professional clothing.

When we entered the office, the Secretary was sitting behind a large desk and smoking an old-fashioned curved pipe. He was jovial, friendly, and asked me many questions about my business plans while listening intently.

Finally, he said, "Nick, you are precisely the kind of man we need in South Africa. You have energy, experience, and drive. You will build businesses and create jobs. We want men like you in our country. I'm not going to send your paperwork to the approval committee. Instead, I will approve it personally. Don't worry about a thing. Welcome to your new home."

Just like that, I was an official resident of South Africa, and I immediately began planning my first business venture, construction on the shopping center project with the commercial property I previously purchased in Phalaborwa. I calculated the project would require about eighteen months to complete. Once that project was finished, we'd move to Durban, a large coastal city Anne and I enjoyed greatly.

To get the Phalaborwa project rolling, I needed to secure one or two national tenants, which would convince lenders to finance the project, even though I'd already paid cash for the land years before. I wrote letters to many potential chains and was delighted to get a letter of intent from Ellerines, a large national retail furniture store. Now that I had my first tenant, I was energized and confident the project would succeed.

I met with architects, construction companies, and financial institutions to gather information and begin planning. I was still looking for a large grocery store as the second anchor tenant.

One day, I went to a grocery store to pick up some things for dinner. The store owner was in the checkout area and struck up a conversation with me, asking if I was new in town. I told him I'd just come from Rhodesia and was preparing to build a shopping center.

We soon discovered we were both from Greece. His name was Yannis, and he was from Pyrgos, near ancient Olympia.

"I love that area! My father took me to run on the track at Olympia when I was just a boy."

"Why don't you come into my office, and we can get to know each other?" Yannis asked.

I really enjoyed our conversation and felt as if I'd found a new friend. Yannis was curious about my plans for the shopping center. He knew a local businessman who wanted to build a shopping center in the same area of town. He wondered if that man might wish to purchase my property and plans. I told Yannis I would be happy to explore any options and offered him a 3 percent commission if a deal came to fruition.

Just two days later, Yannis called and asked me to set a price for my property. The man he knew, Jan, wanted to discuss purchasing the land. Surprisingly, Jan owned the local drive-in cinema in Phalaborwa. We set a meeting a few days later.

Jan and I liked each other very much and realized we'd met before at a cinema convention in Johannesburg. Jan said, "I've been in this town for thirty years. How did you come in, get this land, and secure tenants right under my nose?"

I replied, "Pure luck."

We laughed and started talking about the details of the sale. After Jan had time to review everything, he was happy to purchase my property, plans, and leases. He was pleased I'd done a large portion of the preliminary work, and I was delighted to sell it to him so Anne and I might relocate to Durban right away.

After I completed the deal, I returned to Yannis to give him his commission. He refused the money, saying he was happy to help someone from Greece get a new start in South Africa.

"Oh, no Yannis! You did me a great favor. I want you to have this money. You deserve it."

Yannis took the money, and we shook hands, promising to keep in touch.

Anne and I were excited about moving to Durban, one of the most beautiful cities in South Africa. Durban had beautiful beaches, modern architecture, and world-class surfing, which brought people from all over the world, creating a vibrant city with a strong business economy.

After so many years in land-locked Rhodesia, we relished living on the coast. We said fond farewells to Uncle Willem, Auntie Poppie, and their children, promising to send them plane tickets to visit us in Durban as soon as we got settled.

With the profits from Phalaborwa, we had enough money to cover us while I sought an ideal investment opportunity. We rented a lovely apartment in a high-rise on Durban's North Beach, the most popular part of the city, complete with high-end shops and fine dining, an ice-skating rink, and movie theatres. We saw and heard the crashing waves from our apartment and spent many hours at the beach.

Soon we both recovered from the extreme stress we'd endured over the past two years. I began studying business administration by correspondence course, thinking it would help me with my career goals in Durban. Also, as my custom, I joined a professional soccer team immediately and began networking with the other players, who were very friendly and welcoming.

I was motivated to start establishing a solid business in Durban. My first step was to understand the business environment, which was very different from Rhodesia. Durban was a cosmopolitan city with a long history. Business accounting practices and regulations were much more complicated than any I'd experienced previously. I felt as if I was swimming in a much bigger pond—with many more sharks. I sensed I needed to proceed carefully to ensure my entry into the business arena would be a success.

"Nick, I want my mother to be there when I deliver our baby," Anne said one day later in her pregnancy. "I can't imagine anyone except my mother taking care of me. Please, will you take me to Salisbury for the delivery?"

I dreaded the idea of returning to Rhodesia. The conflict there was still raging and had grown even more intense in the months we'd been in South Africa. Even though I had my residency established in South Africa, I didn't know if it was possible to return to Rhodesia without being arrested. However, I could not deny Anne anything. My love for her was stronger than my concern about returning to Rhodesia. I'd find a way to give her the support she wanted when delivering our baby.

After consultation with Anne's mother, we agreed to drive to Salisbury a few days prior to her delivery date. It was a very long journey from Durban, so we stopped at Phalaborwa to spend a few days with Auntie Poppie and Uncle Willem so Anne could rest.

It was painful for me to return to Rhodesia, reminding me of things I'd seen. However, Anne's comfort was important to me, so I kept those feelings private and focused on our child's arrival.

We were all thrilled when our beautiful daughter Nicolette was born healthy and happy. My heart was full of love from the moment I saw her. Just ten days later, we returned home to Durban, breathing a sigh of relief once we crossed the border into South Africa again.

Baby Nikki inadvertently led me to one of my key business relationships in Durban. I took her with me to a local pharmacy one day and the owner commented on how beautiful she was.

"I'm Henry. Are you new to Durban?" the gentleman asked.

On that day, Henry and I began a life-long friendship. Henry knew Durban astutely, both the business and political systems, and he shared his knowledge freely with me. We enjoyed spending time together discussing business—a passion for both of us. Henry offered to open doors for me and help me find the right business opportunity.

I spent many hours with business brokers looking for opportunities to purchase an existing business. It wasn't easy.

I bid to buy a bus and truck body manufacturing company, but the bid got rejected because I was a new solo investor in Durban.

With that plan down the drain, Henry and I spent many hours together discussing options for my first opportunity. After four months of frustration, I decided to start my own company.

On my many Durban business tours, I'd noticed a few security companies for sale. They were quite profitable but all selling at high prices.

I learned most of the existing security firms were in the suburbs and targeted manufacturing companies. I wanted to be different. I decided we would work near downtown Durban, serving the businesses there and in the nearby port, which was one of the busiest industrial seaports in Africa. It reminded me of Patras but was significantly larger.

With my military background, I believed I could train guards and security officers successfully. It would be a challenge to begin an organization from the ground up, but I relished the opportunity to build infrastructure once again. I'd been waiting long enough. It was time to make my own opportunity.

"That's a wise idea, Nick," Henry said. "Durban is growing, and crime always follows growth. Why don't you name your company Security Services Unlimited? That will give you some room to expand in the future."

I recalled a man I'd known in Rhodesia, David. He'd been a police inspector in the United Kingdom and Rhodesia, then established a successful security company in Fort Victoria. Like me, David moved his family out of Rhodesia, but I wasn't sure where he was. I decided to find David to see if he was willing to become a minority partner in this new business.

It took some detective work, but I found David in Johannesburg. When I contacted him and told him of my plans, he was extremely interested. I bought him a plane ticket to Durban, and he arrived just four days later.

We toured the city and then had a long discussion. David was thrilled about this opportunity. He flew back to Johannesburg and moved his family to Durban just forty-five days later to become my business partner.

David and I moved quickly. We were motivated and willing to do whatever it took to succeed. We agreed David would manage operations and sales while I would be responsible for hiring and training our staff and managing the finances.

To differentiate our company from our competitors, David and I decided to set our guards apart from others in both appearance, professionalism, and training. We selected a smart military-style uniform with dark navy-blue trousers, a lighter blue shirt, and matching jacket, complete with highly polished black boots. This uniform was more striking and professional than other security companies in Durban.

I used a very selective hiring process, seeking men with a strong work ethic, ability to follow procedures, and a willingness to treat everyone with extreme courtesy and respect. Once I hired new recruits, they would complete a rigorous training process, including a full week of paid training where I weeded out any new hires unfit for the position. The training covered physical fitness, communication, grooming, radios and communication equipment, behavior, and emergency preparedness.

Security Services Unlimited secured our first client just six week later, supplying our well-trained guards to a large car dealership. After that, the business grew briskly.

After fifteen months, we started a new division offering guards and highly secure courier services for financial institutions.

My hiring and training processes proved to be remarkably effective. David's professional manner and years of police experience inspired trust, making him the ideal sales leader for our business.

Security Services Unlimited flourished under our joint leadership. Very soon, however, I began to wonder what I might make next.

Chapter 14: Grand Visions Become Real

Anne and I were delighted with our life in Durban. We loved the golden beaches, the crashing waves, and watching the ships in the busy harbor. Now that the security business was running smoothly, we were ready to buy a house. We were most interested in a new suburb, La Lucia, located about ten miles north of Durban.

"That's the one, Nick! That's the house I've been envisioning for years!" Anne said as we drove through the streets of La Lucia one day. Anne was a firm believer in the power of visualization and taught me to use that tool to focus on my business.

Looking at that stunning white contemporary house perched on a manicured lawn, I could also imagine us living there.

We'd never been able to buy our own home, primarily because of the instability in Rhodesia. Yet, we both longed for the security of homeownership and the freedom it provided to decorate and shape a house to our tastes. Plus, we wanted to invest our own money in an asset that would appreciate over time, instead of giving our funds to a landlord every month.

Yet, this house was grander and more expensive than we budgeted for. It had a swimming pool, fountain, large patio, and stunning views of the ocean. It didn't seem to be within our reach. However, I dearly wanted to give Anne the house she dreamed of and so deserved. We set up a tour.

Our realtor told us this house was an excellent buy. At that time, Durban's property prices were depressed, meaning we would get more house for our money.

This house was just five years old and had an interesting story behind it. The owner, Mr. Becker, was an extremely wealthy man. Becker was a professional billiard player and a horse racing bookie with several offices in Durban. He built the house for entertaining, with a huge ground floor easily able to accommodate large crowds. The elegant billiard table, surrounded by seating for spectators, caught my eye immediately.

According to the realtor, Mrs. Becker was tired of hosting large parties at her house every weekend and wanted to move to a penthouse in North Beach facing the ocean.

Anne and I had long discussions about the house. The security business was going well. I was in the process of securing another company and felt confident I could finance the house. Because it was in a prime location and an exclusive and growing suburb, the place was sure to increase in value. I realized we'd make a substantial profit on it if we needed to sell. Buying the house made sense on many levels—as a solid financial investment, and more importantly, as an investment in my family's happiness. There had to be a creative way to acquire it. We decided to go for it and see if we might create a miracle.

We asked our realtor to arrange a meeting with the Beckers. She advised us to bring baby Nikki along because Mrs. Becker loved children, especially little girls. When we arrived, Anne handed

Nikki to Mrs. Becker, who cooed over the baby while we scrutinized the house once again. Then we sat down to talk with the Beckers.

"Mr. and Mrs. Becker, this is the most wonderful house we've seen in Durban. I want you to know we've just arrived here from Rhodesia less than a year ago. I opened a security business here that is very successful. We've been through a lot, and I want to give my beautiful wife Anne and our little girl a magical place to live. This is our dream home. I know I can secure a mortgage. I just need a bit of help with the down payment. Would you be willing to finance half of it with interest for two years?"

The Beckers seemed shocked at my bold request. Mr. Becker said, "We know you've visited our house twice already and can see you are very interested. Let us consider your request and get back to you in a few days."

After we left the house, our realtor was speechless. She'd never had someone make such a bold request. Anne and I believed we could make this happen. We kept visualizing living in the house and talking about how wonderful it would be to own it.

The next day, Mr. Becker called and said, "Nick, you are a young man going places. I feel sorry for anyone who had to go through all that trouble in Rhodesia and want to give you a good start here. If you agree to deliver the money to me in cash with interest, I will finance half of the down payment for you."

We drew up the paperwork and completed the deal. Anne and I were thrilled to move into such a beautiful place. This miraculous event changed my thinking. I now believed anything was possible for me if I visualized it and acted with bold courage. Anne and I decided to visualize our business and life goals regularly from that day forward.

The day we moved into our new home we were filled with so much joy. Little Nikki started toddling around the large rooms while Anne and I walked together behind her.

How proud I was exactly two years later when I slid my automatic pistol into its shoulder harness and put on a sports jacket. I went to the bank, withdrew the cash, and placed it in a briefcase. When I arrived at Mr. Becker's penthouse and rang the bell, he'd forgotten who I was. When I told him I had his money to pay off the financing, he laughed, and we sat down while he counted out all the money and gave me a receipt.

He said, "Something told me you were trustworthy, Nick. You had that look in your eye that told me you were a man of his word. You are going to go far in this town."

It was time to envision expanding my business holdings. By then, I was working with a brilliant CPA, Lionel Sacks, who felt like a brother to me and was always giving me guidance on how to navigate the South African business world. Lionel called me one day with an ideal opportunity. He knew a couple originally from Rhodesia who operated a commercial laundry and dry-cleaning business in Durban. The husband had died, and his overwhelmed widow was looking for a buyer. The firm owned a large commercial laundry and dry-cleaning plant and twenty-five kiosks around the city.

When I went to see the facility, it looked as if it were falling apart. The machinery was old and in poor condition, and even the staff looked worn out and tired. There were many problems with this business, which made it a good opportunity for me if the price was reasonable. When I reviewed the balance sheet on the laundry, I noticed extremely high utility costs. When I visited the location, I saw three old and poorly maintained electric boilers.

I knew I could replace them with a modern coal-fired boiler, producing three times more steam and reducing operating expenses. By paying for the new boiler in installments, I would reap a 100 percent return on investment in less than two years without costly maintenance issues.

As I continued to assess the business, I uncovered several similar opportunities to decrease costs, increase production, and create profits. With a large cash investment and a significant amount of attention from me, I knew this business could become very profitable. I talked everything over with Anne, and we both agreed this was an ideal project for me—a business that needed updating and reorganization in an industry where I had prior experience.

Lionel helped me make a winning offer. The widow accepted, glad to support a new immigrant from Rhodesia and be relieved of a great burden. We agreed I'd take possession of the business in just six weeks.

First, I needed a knowledgeable, trustworthy manager for daily operations, freeing me to focus on improvements. I remembered my old friend Len in Fort Victoria. Len was originally from Durban, so I imagined he'd be eager to return home. When I presented the opportunity to Len and offered to train him, he was delighted to join me in this new venture.

As soon as we took possession of the business, Len and I moved quickly. Within three months, we installed some new equipment and reconditioned the remainder of the machines. Over the next few months, we painted inside and out, installed the new coal-fired boiler, and replaced the factory floor. Next, we remodeled and refreshed all the kiosks.

Our final challenge was the staff. There were forty-five employees when I purchased the business. Some of them refused to follow the new systems and expectations, so they were asked to leave. We hired new, highly motivated staff, eager to follow our directions and contribute to a successful business.

Our goal was to expand capacity, so we installed additional equipment and developed processes to increase speed and efficiency. We introduced a sixty-minute express cleaning service that was very popular. Soon, customers and agents were more satisfied, and the laundry business was gaining a better reputation in Durban.

I was happy to go to work each morning and even happier to arrive home at the end of the day to see Anne and Nikki. Our beautiful home gave me great joy. Family and friends loved gathering there, so we had a steady stream of visitors.

My parents came to see us and were amazed at all we'd created in Durban in just a few short years. By that time, Anne's parents had relocated to South Africa, as well.

Sadly, just as I predicted, my father-in-law lost the gold mine in Rhodesia after a bombing there. We never discussed it or the angry words we had when I was leaving the country, but I worked hard to show him I was providing abundantly for Anne. He never commented, but my mother-in-law's steadfast approval made me glad.

Chapter 15: Raising Higher

The next few years in Durban were full of happiness, expansion, and growth. The security business was thriving with two hundred guards working all around the city, as well as our armored transport for bank assets.

My partner David approached me with a request to purchase my shares of the company. Anne and I discussed it carefully and decided it was a good move. My passion was improving efficiency, customer satisfaction, and profits. Once a business was running smoothly in those three areas, it was time for me to move on to a new opportunity. Selling the security business would free me to devote all my time to improving the laundry.

Len and I were making great strides with the laundry business, securing new commercial contracts, and expanding our retail kiosks around Durban. We instituted a customer rewards program—the first in Durban—where retail customers earned a free cleaning for every five items cleaned.

I also spent a great deal of time working with the staff who served the public. I taught them the customer service techniques my father used in the bakery, greeting repeat customers by name, speaking with great respect, and doing extra things to ensure delighted customers. Our staff had authorization to request an additional cleaning or stain treatment at no cost when needed. Customer service training required a great deal of my time, but it was a very worthwhile investment.

With some of the profits from the sale of the security business, I invested in two residential lots in an area near our home in La Lucia. I had two high-end homes built, which I was able to sell for a nice profit.

I also invested time in making one of my childhood dreams come true. Ever since I'd flown in that shiny, silver Lockheed Super Constellation and seen the cockpit when I was a boy, I longed to become a pilot. When I learned Durban had a few flight schools, my heart leapt, and I enrolled right away.

The instructional program I joined was quite rigorous, requiring fifteen months of classroom instruction and supervised flying time. Some of the instructors were retired British Air Force pilots who were serious about safety and discipline.

I loved every minute of the program. We studied a wide variety of topics, including meteorology, engines, air frames, rules of flight, mechanics, radio communications, navigation, and flight planning. I was surprised to learn how much organization and planning went into each flight. I'd always enjoyed planning, but flight training made me even more meticulous about details.

Each time I went up in a plane with my instructor to practice various techniques, the time passed in a flash. I loved the excitement of ascending into the sky. Because the airport sat near the coast, all planes would execute a 180 degree turn out over the open ocean. It was thrilling to look down and see the blue waters of the Indian Ocean under me and the bright blue sky above me. It felt like Heaven on Earth.

Finally, the day arrived when I made my first solo flight. Anne and Nikki were watching from the viewing area as I soared into the deep blue sky, flying over the ocean and over Durban. I even flew over our house!

While I was deeply thrilled, I had to maintain my focus and follow my flight plan precisely as written. I could not let the excitement of the moment distract me, so I banked my emotions and kept my attention on all my tasks. Only when I completed my landing did my pride and delight bubble up. I could not stop smiling as I exited the cockpit. My happiness grew even deeper when Anne and Nikki celebrated with me.

From that day forward, I flew as often as possible. At first, Anne was a little nervous to fly with me in the small plane. However, I taught her about navigation, which she understood immediately. Once she was involved and serving as the co-pilot doing navigation, she grew to enjoy flying almost as much as I did.

Surprisingly, the skills and tools I learned in flight school exerted a positive influence on my business skills. When flying, I had to make flight plans which was like reverse engineering—another critical business skill. For example, when I needed to fly from Durban to Cape Town, it was a journey of over 1,000 miles. I would begin with the time I needed to arrive in Cape Town and plan all the details of the flight, working backward from that ending point. This type of backward planning has always served me well in business and life. I learned to begin with my goal in mind and then work backward to achieve that goal.

I also enjoyed the way pilots help each other. Good pilots report on the radio dangerous weather encounters, such as hail or heavy turbulence that sometimes the radar doesn't pick up, if they are on the same heading or the same flight level. Fellow pilots, air traffic controllers, and ground crew share information and help you find better ways, like guides for the sky.

From then on, I flew as often as possible, taking family, friends, and business contacts along with me. The trips varied from full-day excursions on Saturdays to short Sunday morning trips, so I'd be back in time for my afternoon soccer games.

Many of Anne's extended family members lived in Durban and they enjoyed flying with me. When my parents came for their next visit, I flew over our house so Mama could see me in the air. She was delighted.

When I returned to the house, she hugged me and laughed, "You always meet your goals, Nico. I don't know how you do it, but there is nothing you can't do when you set your mind to it."

I hoped Mama was right because I was about to take on a huge challenge. In early 1980, my bank manager, Henk, called me about an opportunity.

"Nick, I've learned of an opportunity. You turned the laundry into a profitable business when it was falling apart, so you might be able to fix this business, as well. Two men in Durban have a leather and suede clothing manufacturing plant here in Durban. The business has no debt and is profitable, but the partners argue constantly. They've reached an impasse and decided the only way forward is to sell the company."

My mind immediately started to consider the potential in this business. I got some financial information from Henk and then arranged a factory tour and meeting with the partners. The company had an odd location—ten offices on the twenty-second floor of a high-rise office building in downtown Durban. The company produced good products, very expensive hand-made leather garments which were sold to boutiques around South Africa.

I realized right away the financing partner did not trust his partner enough to invest in much inventory. The company kept little inventory in stock. Instead, they used a wholesale distributor of imported goods who added a thirty percent markup, wasting vast amounts of money.

This situation reminded me of when Cathreen and I purchased my father's bakery and I negotiated with Mr. Hasson to purchase our flour directly from the mills.

After the tour, I began to do additional research and talk with Anne about this opportunity. I had no experience in fashion, yet it seemed my skills in streamlining processes and reducing supply costs, along with my business knowledge, would easily apply to this leather factory. It was easy for me to envision growing this company into a thriving enterprise.

"What do you think, sweetie? Is this something we should do?"

"Yes, sweetie. I believe you can do this. The financial reports look very good. Just think about all the wealthy people in South Africa and all the high-end boutiques here. You should be able to get your products in all those locations."

"I don't really know anything about clothing or fashion, though. That's the only thing that concerns me a bit."

"I'll help you with that part. In fact, I would love to work with the designers. Just imagine me creating a new leather jacket or purse. That would be fun. I can bring Nikki along and we'll become fashion designers!"

We set a goal to grow the company by at least five times its current size. There were many opportunities to improve this business. I smelled the potential.

Lionel, my CPA, helped me structure the deal and take advantage of the tax benefits offered by the South African government. The owners wanted a cash sale, so I negotiated a discount and stipulated that Victor, the owner who managed the design side, would stay with the company for up to twelve months to give me enough time to assemble my own creative team.

As soon as we finished the paperwork, I started planning. My first step was to find a new location. This business needed factory space instead of offices in a high rise. Reducing the rent expenses would create more profit and more space would increase productivity. Because I planned to bring in large quantities of leather, suede, linings, threads, and other notions direct from the manufacturers, I needed a space large enough to store all the material securely and a process for tight inventory control. Buying directly from the manufacturers would generate an additional 33 percent profit.

I found a beautiful and freshly remodeled factory space about a mile away from the current location, and invested in additional renovations, including a loading bay and a large warehouse organized to hold entire containers of leather and suede materials, sorted by color and type. I knew it was essential to prevent theft in any manufacturing business, so I created robust processes to secure materials and tightly monitor inventory.

Next, I purchased the latest machines to decrease the need for intense manual labor. The previous owners did much of the stitching, fusing, button-making, and cutting by hand instead of using machinery, driving up their costs, and limiting production. To reach my growth goals, I would mechanize and modernize all aspects of production.

Once the machines arrived and the factory was arranged in an attractive, organized, and streamlined manner, we started production. In time, I invited all the sales representatives to come to Durban and tour the new facility. During the event, I asked them for their ideas on improving the business and the product line.

Kurt, the representative from Johannesburg, spoke first. "Do you really want our input? I gave suggestions to Victor many times and he never listened. If you will take us seriously, we can tell you precisely what the store owners and customers want."

"Thank you, Kurt. I want to hear all your suggestions. If we all work together, we can grow this company. You'll all make more sales and reap much higher commissions. I'm always interested in your ideas. In fact, I depend on them to help us succeed," I replied.

The meeting went very well. Having the support of the sales staff, and a steady flow of customer information, helped us plan our new products.

The next twelve months were intense. I found an Italian pattern maker who worked in Hollywood but recently relocated to Durban. I built a full new design team with experience in leather and suede production. My new factory manager had thirty years of experience in Durban's clothing production, so he understood the culture and employee mindset.

Next, I found new suppliers for our fabrics and notions. Because I had cash reserves, I was able to buy in bulk and greatly reduce our costs. We used suede and leather produced in South Africa, supplemented by leathers, snakeskin, and other exotic fabrics from all over the world. I even found manufacturers in Japan and Italy who produced high-quality man-made leather and suede, which were washable and breathable, more suitable for South Africa's warm climates.

We expanded our inventory, always with a focus on high quality and unique garments. It was challenging because designs changed every six months for winter and summer orders, which meant we needed new styles, colors, and options to interest boutique owners every six months. I created a separate design team focused entirely on developing new samples, including fit models, designers, pattern makers and graders, and machinists.

Anne spent a great deal of time working the new design team, even arranging fashion shows for the sales staff and key customers. She was a wonderful seamstress and able to offer many useful ideas. While she devoted a tremendous amount of attention to Nikki, she enjoyed contributing to the business as well. Every evening we'd talk about the business and ways to improve it. I was so fortunate to have Anne's keen mind on my side.

However, Anne was giving me more than great business ideas. In 1981, she gave me a son. I was so proud to name him Panagioti, after my father, the most influential man in my life. Four-year-old Nikki instantly fell in love with little Pany and delighted in watching over him. She became a devoted big sister, just like my sister Cathreen had been to me.

It was beautiful to watch Anne as a mother. She was so kind, nurturing, and encouraging. While she might have had an important career, she chose to devote all her intelligence and energy to our children. They thrived under her loving attention.

As the leather business expanded, I began to send my designers and sales agents to leather and suede clothing shows in Europe, which allowed us to stay current with fashion trends and pricing as well as network with buyers from the most exclusive boutique chains. We were the premier producer of mass-produced leather clothing in South Africa as well as shipping coats and garments for European distribution in large department store chains. Surprisingly, our garments made of the washable suede were innovative and remarkably successful, especially in the European market.

The leather business gave me my first taste of working in an international marketplace. I was, and continue to be, passionate about the constant need for innovation and new processes. Even though I had the factory running like clockwork, it had to be changed every six months, which allowed me the opportunity to solve new challenges. It was an extremely satisfying business. In time, I met our goal, increasing the profitability of the business by five times.

I was proud to produce custom leather coats for my family. I had two long coats of beautiful, soft leather made for my mother, who looked so beautiful in them my father joked another man would steal her away from him. Cathreen also took a beautiful coat home with her after a visit to Durban.

My cousin Maki from Greece, now a ship captain like his father, began shipping goods to Durban. He came to visit me every time he was in Durban. It was wonderful to see him after so many years.

Maki was amazed I was producing goods of such high quality. He told me my garments were better than any available in Greece. We made a beautiful coat for his wife. It made me proud to think of a woman in Kefalonia wearing a coat made in my factory in South Africa.

I'd heard some say life was a circle. With all the expansion of our leather goods to Europe and my connection back to Greece through my cousin's visits, I believed it.

Chapter 16: The Seeds of Doubt

In 1992, I received a surprising letter from my brother, Peter. While I did not follow politics in Rhodesia closely, I knew the Rhodesian government had been dissolved. My old passenger, Robert Mugabe, was elected the Prime Minister of the newly formed Zimbabwe.

Dear Nico,

I was recently invited to the governmental palace in Harare, the new name for Salisbury, at the invitation of Prime Minister Mugabe. I was mystified. During the meeting Mugabe thanked me for providing him with transportation in the Zimba Reserve. I realized he must have been referring to you. I never drove a van in Zimba.

I guess because we look so much alike, Mugabe had no idea he was speaking to the wrong brother. I just listened. Mugabe invited me to join his government! I am now the representative of the remaining white population. I do not agree with many of Mugabe's policies, but I did not believe it would have been safe to refuse him.

Nico, it felt very strange for me to take this post, knowing it was meant for you. I am unsure of what the future will hold for us in the new Zimbabwe, but I believe having this position will help me save the bakery and my other assets.

Thank you, my brother.

I had extremely mixed emotions about Peter's letter. I still carried some sorrow from the loss of the Coronet and my life in Rhodesia, even though I was extremely happy in South Africa.

My remaining family there weathered the turbulent governmental changes, although life in the new Zimbabwe was quite different for them. Peter now owned the bakery after my father retired.

At least now that the conflict was over, I'd be able to visit them more regularly without fear of being arrested as a deserter. I hoped Mugabe would be a wise leader and protect all the people there.

It was clear conditions throughout Africa were changing rapidly, including in South Africa. My CPA and good friend Lionel decided to move to the United States and urged me to leave South Africa before violence erupted. Many other businessmen began to leave, as well.

Anne and I discussed our future in South Africa regularly. We had a wonderful life in Durban full of friendships and profitable businesses. We loved living near her family and being a part of such a loving clan.

On the other hand, we both carried scars from our dangerous exit from Rhodesia and never wanted to be in a similar position in the future, especially now that we had Nikki and Pany to consider.

We decided to proceed cautiously and monitor conditions in South Africa carefully. If we had to leave South Africa, we both agreed to move to the United States, believing our children would have strong opportunities there. As a first step, we'd begin visiting the USA on vacations making our first trip there in 1984.

While we kept our eyes on the stability of South Africa, I had a new business opportunity, but was unsure I wanted to pursue it. Durban was growing, with a newly constructed train and bus station in the northern part of the city. Directly across the street, there was a large minimarket and takeout food business for sale, Tony's Food World.

I felt doubtful about this opportunity when my business broker approached me with it. From my past food business experience, I knew these businesses required knowledgeable and experienced management. I didn't know anyone in Durban who would be able to fill those roles. But the broker said he would connect me with honest and professional people, so I decided to tour the operation.

The business had an excellent location and great foot traffic, serving up to one hundred chicken dinners each day to hungry travelers. I was interested in the colossal refrigeration room at the back, almost the size of a shipping container. About fifty people worked on-site in two shifts from 6 a.m. to 10 p.m., seven days a week.

After the tour, I interviewed each of the potential managers the broker recommended and liked each of them very much. My favorite was a younger man named Morgan. He was a family man, intelligent and fit, with several good ideas for improving the business. His work ethic and enthusiasm impressed me.

After researching the opportunity, my gut told me this business would be a worthwhile investment. Because of the location, I believed I could streamline operations and make it more profitable.

By that time, I had few responsibilities at the laundry business. I spent a great deal of time working in the leather factory but felt it would be possible to add this food business to my portfolio if I brought in excellent managers.

"Sweetie, thank you for reviewing all these financial statements! What do you think about buying Food World?" I asked, as Anne had become my most trusted advisor and confidant in our life together. I couldn't even dream of making a decision without her input.

"Well, the financials are sound, and the location is fantastic. Sweetie, I think we should buy it. You can make it a big success."

We made all our business decisions together. While I was the public face of our business concerns, we were always a team. Anne provided the sounding board, wise counsel, and encouragement I needed to set big goals and achieve them.

Food World was on my way home from the leather factory, making it easy to stop by for a short time each day to ensure things were going well. I used to spend each Friday afternoon there and worked at one of the six cash registers. It was fun to serve customers and talk to them—like I had in the family stores in Rhodesia. I also hired an employee to monitor each item's daily sales, check inventory, and report to me at my office in the leather factory.

With improvements, we were able to increase sales by 20 percent. My focus was on customer service and increasing speed. We served our food faster than our competitors and with great respect, leading to many repeat customers. These changes were successful, and the sales continued to grow each year. Over time we purchased two similar businesses at the two other train stations in Durban.

While I was pleased with the food businesses, I realized they didn't excite me as much as manufacturing did. I relished improving machinery and process flow, harkening back to my days in the bakery with my father. The lessons I learned there guided me to success.

Because we had such successful businesses, Anne and I started a series of renovations and improvements in our house. She had a fantastic design sense and regularly developed ideas for making our beautiful home even more comfortable and lovely.

I could hardly wait to come home to my well-organized and beautiful home each night. Anne and the children would greet me at the door with hugs and kisses, filling my heart with gratitude.

During that time, I met other business owners who seemed to avoid their families, spending too many hours at work or in bars. Their behavior did not make sense to me at all. My family and home were a source of strength and happiness, not a burden. Because a loving family supported me, I had boundless energy and optimism to set new goals in the business arena.

When I wasn't at home or at work, I continued my involvement with soccer. After a few years, I aged out of playing professionally, so I joined a recreational league as a player and coach.

I coached the boys soccer team at Nikki's school. Pany loved kicking the soccer ball around with me almost as soon as he could walk. When he was old enough to play, I coached his team as well.

During these years, I continued to fly every week. I was passionate about flying, and was meeting many wonderful people including commercial pilots, captains flying for South African Airways and a large cadre of private pilots, physicians, businessmen, accountants, attorneys, and engineers who all shared my passion for flight. There was something special about people who flew planes, and I found many wonderful friends in that community.

In time, I formed a corporation with three other businessmen I'd met flying. One was an attorney; another owned a large Mercedes Benz distributorship, and the third owned an aluminum smelting business. We pooled our funds and purchased an aircraft together, taking turns using it for personal and business purposes.

My partners and I eventually built our fleet to three planes. Our largest plane seated ten passengers. In time, we leased our planes for flights within South Africa to government and other commercial pilots if they passed my screening process. I was cautious to only lease planes to excellent commercial pilots who were very safe.

My partners and I rotated the business' functions, including accounting and scheduling, but I always took responsibility for approving new pilots.

Having our own planes was a boon for business, saving me time and giving me a great deal of flexibility. I flew all over Southern Africa on business trips, which was much more efficient than flying commercial or driving. When I had large deliveries of leather goods, it was quicker to fly than deliver them on trucks.

I also deepened my relationships with colleagues through flying. I took friends on many trips for fishing, day trips, and longer trips to explore the rest of Africa. My banker, Henk, my accountant, Gary, my good friends, Henry and Len, my parents, and siblings, and even Durban's mayor enjoyed many trips with me, as did my business partners and managers and countless others. I also organized day trips for professional pilots who had long layovers in Durban and wanted to see the surrounding area. We also flew on family vacations whenever possible.

I flew to Mozambique, Zimbabwe, Namibia, Botswana, and Swaziland and several islands in the Indian Ocean over the years. These flights were a bit risky because many of the countries lacked repair facilities or replacement parts.

One day, I set a speed record for the type of aircraft I flew for flying 1,200 miles nonstop from northwest Namibia to Durban.

Some of my fellow pilots started racing their planes, but I never did, even though I had set that record. I was having too much fun flying people around for fun and for my business.

Once I was coming into the Durban airport from a neighboring country with a plane full of passengers. Suddenly, I realized the undercarriage of the plane was not descending properly. I couldn't land without the wheels locked into place, so I notified air traffic control in Durban and asked them for clearance to fly over the tower so they could use binoculars to see if my wheels were down. They reported the wheels were down, but they couldn't confirm whether they were locked in place.

Landing without that lock might destroy the bottom of the plane, start a fire, or cause a terrible accident. I notified the passengers to put their seatbelts on and started procedures with my co-pilot to use a hand crank and pump the hydraulics manually to lock the wheels. This is a very time-consuming procedure.

The biggest risk in a landing like this was fire. If the plane scraped the runway, sparks would ignite the fuel, causing the plane to explode.

My first task was to fly out over the sea to burn off as much excess fuel as possible, giving me time to create a plan while the co-pilot cranked the emergency hydraulic wheel lock to get the wheels in place for landing. My flight training prepared me for all sorts of emergencies, so I followed the rules of flight and stayed calm, even though it was a potentially dangerous situation.

After I burned as much fuel as possible, I prepared the passengers for an emergency landing, instructing them to exit the plane and run from it as soon as we stopped moving. I would wait and exit the plane only after everyone disembarked safely. The captain always protects his passengers. The wheels started to come down from the hand cranking, but the instrument panel was still red, alerting me our landing could be difficult.

The tower personnel got firetrucks and ambulances ready for our landing. They also closed the airport so no other planes would be landing as we came in. But my co-pilot and I stayed calm and worked through all the emergency procedures.

When I turned the plane to begin the final approach, I switched the engines off about fifty feet above the runway, ensuring the propeller blades were at their highest position to protect them as much as possible if the main wheels collapsed. I turned off all the lights to ensure nothing sparked. Then, I instructed the co-pilot to switch off the fuel lines as soon as I switched off the engines to prevent a possible fire.

As we touched down as gently as I could manage, the main wheels held. I knew then we were going to be okay. I was so thankful I landed the plane safely, without damage to my passengers or the aircraft. My engineers later discovered a cracked monitor switch near the undercarriage caused the problem.

Other flying experiences were more humorous. Once, I took eight of my friends to Northwest Namibia for a fishing and safari vacation. We stopped at Fort Namutoni, located in a very remote area without an air control tower.

Fort Namutoni, formerly a German military fort, was now a large hotel with a game park full of wild animals surrounded by high walls. When planes arrived, the procedure was to fly twice over the Fort and pull the throttles back and forth to create a different engine sound signal. Hotel staff would hear the sound and send a bus to the unmanned airstrip about four miles from the hotel compound. I called the day before our arrival to confirm our arrival time with the staff.

Many airstrips in the remote areas of Africa consist of a dirt road or strip of tarmac in the middle of the wilderness. Before landing, I usually had to fly low to ensure there were no wild animals on the runway. If there were animals present, I'd have to fly over them full throttle very low with the undercarriage and flaps extended down to maximum to get them to move out of the area. Our landing on that day was animal-free and went perfectly.

Then, we realized the hotel bus was not coming, even though we'd waited a long time in the hot Kalahari Desert sun. There were no cellphones in those days, so we had no way of contacting the hotel. After thirty minutes, we decided to walk down the road, knowing we'd eventually come to the hotel, and after a long walk, we arrived at the large metal gates around the compound.

The armed guards could not believe we walked there. They said area was full of lions, cheetahs, baboons, hyenas, buffalos, elephants, and other wild animals. We might have easily been attacked and eaten. When I told them we were from Durban, they laughed, saying, "You guys from the big cities have no idea what is going on in the wild."

Flying in Africa was always an adventure. In Botswana, I learned pilots must put wild thorn bushes tightly around their tires when parking planes overnight. If not, hyenas will eat the tires.

I had to stay alert and be prepared for anything, whether it was the challenge of landing on remote landing strips, the wild animals ready to greet us, or the intense storms making journeys unpredictable and somewhat dangerous.

Chapter 17: A Diamond in the Rough

Even though I was concerned about our future in South Africa, I was still expanding my life and holdings. Most importantly, we had another beautiful baby, a little girl we named Athena.

I was so grateful to be a business owner instead of an employee at a business. While I was extremely busy at work, I had the flexibility I needed to spend as much time with my family as I wished. Somehow, I found a way to balance my time between my family, my businesses, soccer, and flying. I was a busy and fortunate man.

After seven years, my manager in the laundry business, Len, and I decided it was time to sell it. It was extremely profitable, but both of us were eager to take on new challenges. We easily found a buyer who offered us three times the total I'd invested in the business. Len and I happily parted ways. While we would not work together in business any longer, we'd always remain dear friends. I used some of those profits to invest in three small manufacturing businesses.

One day, my brother-in-law, Phil, called me. "Hey Nick, I have a business you might want to buy. It's right up your alley. It's called Hawkins and they make battery chargers. I hear they are having some problems meeting customer demand."

Whenever I would form relationships with people, I'd share my passion for business growth. Because my friends and relatives knew what kind of businesses I enjoyed buying, it was easy for them to pass along opportunities. They knew I'd gladly pay them a commission on a successful purchase, so they were motivated to find opportunities.

Phil knew I loved helping manufacturing businesses increase production output and streamline processes. It is what I had become known for, earning me the nickname "Mr. Fix-It."

A few days later, I visited Hawkins, had an impromptu meeting with Lenard, the owner. I told Lenard a bit about my work and that I was interested in buying his business directly, without involving any brokers or agents. Lenard told me he might consider selling if the price was right. He agreed to have his accountant draw up current financials and have a second meeting to discuss them.

The factory was an awful mess. It was located on the third floor of an old, dirty building without elevators. The factory floor was an overwhelming, chaotic muddle of old inventory and discarded equipment piled haphazardly around the working equipment. There were no straight pathways anywhere due to all the junk. Worse yet, it was full of dust and dirt.

The factory reminded me of a depressing junkyard. This excited me. I could clearly envision the potential of this place if it were reorganized, cleaned, and retooled with modern equipment.

The more I spoke with Lenard, I realized he was a skillful electrician and innovator but a poor businessman. He lacked the organizational and process skills to grow the company.

Additionally, Lenard seemed uninterested in Hawkins. He spent little time there because of his commitments in his other business. I became more and more excited about the potential in this company.

In our next meeting, I reviewed additional financial information. It appeared the business had a skillful accountant who kept the books in good order. Lenard quoted me a price, but it was much higher than I expected based on the profit ratios, but I was not deterred.

"So, Lenard, tell me about your partner Greg." I asked.

"Greg is a great guy. I've known him since he was a boy. He's honest, dependable, and very hardworking. He's married and has a couple of children, so he's very stable."

"Well, that sounds good. Is he responsible for opening and closing? How about ordering materials and working with suppliers?"

As I probed for more information, I was trying to learn how much responsibility Greg carried for daily operations and finances. Lenard's words revealed Greg was essentially running the business while Lenard focused on creating new products. My experience taught me that buying a business with a motivated and experienced leader was a recipe for success, so I was quite interested in talking with Greg.

Greg got excited when I reviewed my plans for Hawkins, which included moving to a larger, cleaner factory on the ground floor, revising and streamlining all production, and expanding into new products. I believed Greg would become a valuable employee if he would stay with me after the sale.

When I asked him, Greg looked me square in the eyes and said, "Nick, I've wanted to make these kinds of changes for years. Our customers keep asking us for more products, but Lenard isn't interested. No one likes working in this depressing mess. It will be a lot of work, but I'd love to help you transform Hawkins into a successful business."

I went home that night, full of excitement about the potential in Hawkins. It certainly had a lot of problems, but they were problems I knew I would solve. My mind became very eager to begin fixing this company. There was enormous potential to streamline production, create additional products and move into exporting.

Based on my experience with the leather factory, I anticipated expanding into many new markets with the Hawkins products. Hawkins would require a large investment in time, equipment, and thought, but was sure to bring me a solid return on investment. It was a great challenge—and I loved business challenges.

During our third meeting, Lenard and I reached an agreement, and the sale went forward smoothly. He agreed to stay on for a while as an advisor for the research and development team, working on developing new products customers had requested.

Greg and I got busy clearing the chaos and the plant.

Our first step was to clear the chaos. There was so much junk we sent two fully loaded, ten-ton trucks to the scrapyard, which provided the space for a locked parts storeroom and rearranging the machines to speed up production. I began to purchase all supplies directly from the manufacturers in bulk, decreasing costs by 30 percent. Because we were able to make products faster, production increased by 25 percent, and we finally cleared the long list of backorders.

Next, Greg and I began to build inventory for more rapid delivery in the future. The R&D team completed the pending four new battery charger models, so we had enough models to cover most of the needs for our existing clients.

Once I optimized production, it was time to create a strategic marketing plan. My initial goal centered on the South African market, followed by international exporting. Greg and I met with all our South African distributors, sharing our plans for high quality, new products. When we announced special pricing deals so the distributors might penetrate their local markets, they became very enthusiastic.

To further support them, we sent our repairmen out to all the distributors to provide free training to complete simple repairs on any chargers, even providing them with the required parts. It was easier and cheaper for them to do small repairs locally, so they did not have to ship chargers back to our factory. We even established a hot line to supply immediate help with repair problems.

The distributors were delighted with all these improvements which enabled them to sell more products. Orders increased rapidly.

Next, it was time to branch out. I sent a few members of my staff overseas to check out our competition, especially in Europe. The South African government had a program to fund exhibits at international trade shows and offered attractive tax incentives for exporting. So, we registered Hawkins Manufacturing as an exporter and brought in additional research and development teams to create new chargers for global markets, including those for yachts, motorcycles, cars, buses, motorhomes, and heavy equipment.

Our first show was the Automechanika trade show in Frankfurt, Germany. The show attracted automobile component manufacturers from around the world. We took eight different models with us—a pallet full of equipment, which the South African government paid to transport for us.

Greg and I attended the show and learned much during the five-day event. We realized our products were superior to most of the competition's battery chargers because of their sturdy construction and toroidal transformers, which made them extremely dependable. We left Frankfurt energized and determined to bring a more extensive, improved inventory to the show the following year. Hawkins was ready to enter the global marketplace.

Unfortunately, I was struggling to find a good location for the factory, even after searching for almost two years. Our current location lacked parking and was in a seedy part of town. One of our trucks was stolen right from our parking lot. We had distributors and visitors coming in regularly and I hated to bring them to an unsafe part of town. I wanted them to be impressed by our facilities.

So, I developed the grandest plan I'd ever envisioned. At the time, the city of Durban was developing a new upscale industrial park, Springfield Park. I toured the area and found a parcel of four conjoined lots in an excellent location. I decided to buy them all and create factory space for eight companies. This plan would allow me to house Hawkins and my three other small manufacturing companies in the same location, plus build out four other rental sites. I've always believed in going big, and I felt the time was ripe to take on a large-scale project and go as big as I possibly might.

Every night after the children were asleep, Anne and I would discuss the project.

"What do you think, Sweetie? Is this risk too big for us?" I asked.

"Sweetie, nothing is too big for us if we believe we can do it. Remember when we thought this house was out of our reach? We made that happen. Every time we set a goal; we achieve it. Do you really want this?"

"Yes, I do. I've always wanted to put my four manufacturing businesses all under one roof. It takes me so long to drive around to visit them all now. Besides, Baba taught me it was always wise to own your building site, so you didn't have to answer to a landlord," I replied.

"Alright, then, sweetie, let's start visualizing this plan coming into reality. I support you 100 percent."

I could always count on Anne's belief in me. It was particularly important now that I was embarking on the biggest project of my career.

I began a comprehensive analysis of the financial implications for this project. While I was in Durban, I'd only rented commercial property. As my businesses expanded, I'd have to move locations, incurring additional expenses, spending extra time, and lost production time. If I owned commercial property, I would be able to construct factories that would meet my precise specifications and have plenty of room for expansion.

The tax structure allowed me to deduct mortgage payments, property tax, and other related expenses, so becoming an owner would not increase my tax burden. Additionally, the commercial real estate market in Durban was growing. If I purchased the property now, it would appreciate, becoming an asset for the future.

Fortunately, while I was researching and planning for this expansion, a buyer approached me about acquiring the leather factory. At that point, we'd owned it for ten years. I was incredibly proud of it because of our innovation and successful expansion into international markets. At the same time, I believed I'd grown it as far as possible. As my energy was always drawn to expansion, not just maintaining a business, it seemed like an ideal time to sell the leather business and devote my time to my new dreams.

My architects drew up plans for a state-of-the-art facility. I instructed them to include the most sophisticated security monitoring screens, a well-organized loading dock system, and beautiful factory spaces for eight companies with thirty-foot-high ceilings so each company could expand to a mezzanine floor and grow without relocating.

The other companies in the park housed very high-end research and development organizations, so my building needed to be as attractive as possible to fit into the development, with quality materials and a pleasing aesthetic. I named the complex Springhawk, a combination of Hawkins and Springfield Park. The plans looked very impressive.

Once they were completed, it was time to get some feedback from my business advisors. I did a presentation for Henk and a few of my other advisors. Everyone was very enthusiastic.

I discussed this idea with Anne, who immediately saw the potential in this plan. Then, I talked with Henry, Greg, and some of my other trusted advisors to get their feedback. Everyone was enthusiastic, especially Henry, who'd been my first business supporter in Durban in 1977 and continued to give me sage advice.

However, when I approached my bank for construction financing, they were reluctant to take on such a big project until I had signed tenant leases for the rental sites. The bank wanted to finance half of the project immediately and then finance the remainder in the following year, significantly increasing my costs. I was not satisfied with this plan at all.

My old friend, Henk, the banker who helped me establish my first businesses in Durban, had become a close friend over the years. Our families traveled together, I'd take Henk with me on airplane trips regularly, and we often had lunch together and attended sporting events.

During the twelve years of our friendship, Henk's career at the bank soared. He was now a top official working on the very highest floor of the bank building. In all our years of friendship, I'd never asked Henk for a favor, but now I needed his help.

When I called Henk, he asked me to send him all the plans and estimates for the project. After he reviewed the paperwork and we discussed everything, Henk invited the loan manager, officers, and me to a meeting in his office.

He said, "Look, I've known Nick for twelve years and observed him carefully. Everything he touches turns to gold. I know he can succeed with this project. I will write a letter in support of this loan."

Henk's support ensured I got full financing for my project. I was overjoyed!

Now that the financing was in place, I wanted to move rapidly to construct the complex. The lease agreements on Hawkins and one of my other businesses were coming due and I did not want to renew them. Construction costs were also increasing so it was prudent to move quickly and complete Springhawk as soon as possible. I paid additional fees in overtime to ensure the contractor would complete everything in just eight months. We'd all be working with an incredibly demanding schedule, but I was certain it was necessary for our success.

The next eight months would be intense as I juggled Hawkins's demands with my other businesses, the construction project, and my family. I visited the construction site twice each day and did everything possible to hasten the construction. The extra overtime costs would be easily recouped once we were in the new location and able to expand production.

Unfortunately, during construction of the new complex, representatives from the Industrial Metal and Electrical Union arrived at the original Hawkins factory informing Greg most of our production employees wanted to join the union. We were shocked. Our staff were already receiving well above market wage and enjoyed excellent working conditions.

I would not tolerate being bullied by disgruntled employees when I'd worked so hard to ensure working at Hawkins was a very positive experience. There was no need for a union to interfere with my business. I was also concerned that if Hawkins employees unionized, my other three businesses would follow suit, making them all less valuable.

After consultation with some other business owners in Durban, I devised a win-win solution. We'd shift to a new model of independent contractors instead of employees, then pay a high piece rate for work completed. In that way, the contractors would be able to earn up to 40 percent additional pay, and we'd have an even more motivated team.

This situation added stress to an already busy time with the construction and factory move. However, it was imperative for me to retain authority over my own business and ensure its profitability.

While Greg and I planned the roll out of the independent contractor model, I also had to plan for a smooth transition to our new location, ensuring we had surplus inventory so none of our distributors would experience delays in fulfilling orders. We also needed to communicate the plans about our new location and expanded capabilities clearly so our distributors knew we'd take good care of them during the transition. I also encouraged them to place orders early so we'd have less stock to move to the new location.

It was a Herculean effort to manage all these details amid a major construction project. I thought constantly about all the details and kept a careful eye on all my plans and projections.

The ninety days leading up to the relocation were some of the most challenging of my career as I juggled the needs of the contractors, staff, distributors, and clients. However, I felt energized making everything happen. I loved living life without limits.

Chapter 18: Roll Out the White Carpet

———————————————————➤

"Welcome, ladies and gentlemen, to the grand opening of Durban's most exciting new industrial complex, Springhawk!" Henry boomed out a welcome to enthusiastic applause.

Henry, my first friend in Durban, was now the mayor of our city, and just as supportive of me as ever.

He continued, "This complex, the creation of Nick and Anne Haritatos, brings the latest technology to Durban and is certain to grace our city with new jobs and continued prosperity. Congratulations, Nick and Anne, as well as all your employees who made this grand opening possible."

The Hawkins factory floor was full of linen-covered banquet tables and fresh flowers. A band played in front of a large dance floor, and as I looked out over the room, I could see two hundred happy faces.

Henk, my banking friend, was there, along with Greg and his wife. Our customers, suppliers, and distributors came from all over

South Africa to attend our grand opening gala, along with other friends from my soccer teams and flying colleagues, and the managers from all my businesses. The most important guests were Anne, the children, and our relatives from South Africa.

My heart was bursting with pride. We'd completed the Springhawk factory complex in just eight months.

Now, it was time to celebrate! After Henry's remarks, Anne and I took the children out to the dancefloor. Anne held little Athena in her arms while I danced her around the floor, Nikki and Pany dancing together nearby. My heart was filled with deep pride as I watched my beautiful family dance.

"Come, join us everyone," I urged.

Soon the floor was full of dancers, enjoying the music and beautiful location.

We had a grand party. Anne gave me a special gift, singing a solo with the band in my honor. She'd taken singing lessons for years and had a lovely voice but never performed in public. I got tears in my eyes watching her sing, especially for me.

Later in the evening I joined the band, playing the drums for a few songs, putting my music lessons from Gatooma into good use. It was a night to remember!

The Springhawk complex was more beautiful than I imagined with a sleek and modern design developed for efficiency. Constructed in an open U-shape, the complex featured loading docks in the center and the reception on the opposite side. I planned each detail meticulously with thirty-foot ceilings, epoxy floors, air conditioning, lots of windows and natural light, and a sophisticated sound system for music inside and outdoors.

One of my other businesses generated thousands of dollars in cash each day when drivers returned from delivering food products to stores. To protect it, I created a large cash vault that was as secure as a large bank's, with walls that could withstand bomb blasts. When someone wanted to enter the complex, they were first screened by a guard at the gate, then again before entering the reception area.

My years in the security business gave me the expertise required to provide a very safe environment. I also installed the best security systems available, with cameras, heavy security doors, and full-time guards working around the clock. Because of the increasing crime in Durban at the time, I wanted to ensure the safety of my staff and tenants, as well as all our combined equipment, and merchandise.

My office became one of my favorite features in the new complex. Visitors said it looked like the command center from Star Trek. It was high above the factory floor in the center of the complex. It featured glass walls on three sides with large sliding glass doors so I could see the workings of three of the businesses from my office. I had beautiful metal stairways from my office that would allow me to walk down to any of my three factories. It was full of security monitors to view the loading docks and both the inside and outside the buildings.

I installed beautiful furniture and white carpet in my office. Everyone who entered my office for the first time was amazed. No one else would put white carpet in a factory. That white carpet was a symbol of cleanliness, organization, and innovation. Each time I entered my office, I slipped off my shoes in respect for the ideals represented by that white carpet.

After that magical party, it was time to move Hawkins to the new factory complex. The move went smoothly, using a color-coding and numbering system I'd developed in previous business moves. Every item was carefully labeled and coded so it could be immediately placed in its new location. Because everything was so well organized, we were able to move the factory quickly. Production at the new location started just ten days after we left the old site.

Once production began at Hawkins, we worked vigilantly to ensure all the new processes worked well, troubleshooting any issues quickly. My plan for piecework payments required careful analysis of each component of all the battery chargers, welding machines, the fabrication time, and assembly time for all the models on each production line. We broke everything down and listed each battery charger, welding machine model, the other related products, and each required component. Then we tested the fabrication and assembly with several independent contractors to set a fair time estimate. I was excited about how this new system would motivate staff to work at capacity and control their earnings.

However, this new system emphasizing speed had the potential to create quality problems. I did not want to jeopardize our good name and reputation, which is of utmost importance in business, so I decided to develop new quality control positions, also staffed by independent contractors, who would do nothing but testing and quality monitoring. Low quality on their line would result in less pay for the quality control monitor. In this way, everyone was motivated by the opportunity to earn.

Our new approach increased our production capacity significantly. Within three months in the new location, we were making 30 percent more profit. The contractors were clear about how much they wanted to earn each week and precisely what was required to reach their goals.

Hawkins was operating smoothly and growing well. Greg and I were delighted to see our plans coming to life so successfully.

While I was moving Hawkins, I also found tenants for the remaining four factories. Potential tenants were impressed with the security of the complex and the high ceilings which provided space for expansion. The complex was fully leased just three months after our opening day celebration.

During this time, I also moved my other three businesses to the new complex. The first, Coastal Sun Food Prepackers, was the brainchild of Anne's brother-in-law, Douglas, who had experience in milling and agricultural products. We formed a company and purchased locally grown cornmeal and beans in bulk directly from the farmers, as well as imported rice from overseas, then packaged them for resale.

This business required giant hoppers holding over a ton of product each, as well as forklifts and weighing and packaging machines. Our machines would package and label the foods in different sized heavy plastic bags to distribute to wholesale and national brand name grocery stores. This business needed room for expansion, so I moved it beside the Hawkins factory. Both companies used the new loading bays, which could load or offload a thirty-ton truck in about thirty minutes. The extra space and additional equipment led to an expansion in sales and profit for that food packaging business.

The next business of mine in the new complex manufactured aluminum windows, doors, and related products. It also had a division that provided installation for both commercial and residential properties.

Some years earlier, I had purchased the well-established business and kept the staff. Aki, the manager, had excellent ideas for expansion. This company only needed more space, a streamlined production flow, and new computer programs to design the most modern doors and windows. After moving to Springhawk, it became almost an autopilot operation under Aki's excellent supervision. Sales grew an average of 35 percent each year.

My final business was an exciting challenge for me. I purchased a dormant company that was supposed to be manufacturing motorized wheelbarrows capable of carrying up to one thousand pounds of materials. Initially designed in France, these machines were ideal for South Africa. They replaced six men, could maneuver in tight spaces, and were safe for operation inside underground mines. However, the original owners just dumped all the components in a warehouse and took no further action for a few years. They were happy to sell everything to me.

It was like buying a puzzle. We had to find all the pieces and jigs to construct prototypes—which engaged my engineering mind—locate sources for all the components, including those made overseas, then create efficient assembly processes, and educate the market regarding the usefulness of this new technology.

We named the machine Loadrunner and developed a very high-quality product after testing several prototypes. After we demonstrated it at several trade shows in both South Africa and overseas, sales began coming in briskly. After eighteen months, profits overtook losses. We also designed a snowplow attachment that was extremely popular in nations with winter snows.

I loved going to work each day. From my wonderful office, I could monitor everything easily and visit each of my companies daily. I was delighted with the managers working in each organization. It made me proud to provide a beautiful workplace with beautiful, exciting, motivating music and comfortable conditions for the staff and to give so many the ability to feed their families and have a good life.

My practice was to always be visible in each of my businesses, greeting staff warmly and walking around. I was friendly yet commanded respect. Maintaining respect was crucial in such a large and busy organization. I carefully cultivated respect by always being fair and rewarding good work, yet never allowing any violation of the simple rules: no stealing, work hard, and use patience and respect, especially with customers.

When someone was underperforming, our policy was for the manager to talk with them about it once to ensure they understood expectations. No improvement meant no further work. South Africa had rampant unemployment, so almost everyone valued and appreciated their positions.

My time with the military taught me the importance of a clear chain of command. I trained my managers to deal with problems first and to come to me if they needed help. In that way, the workers took their ideas and issues to their managers first.

Whenever we had big orders and needed extra efforts, I would meet with the team, tell them about the opportunity, and ask them how we could meet the customer's needs. They would volunteer for extra shifts, creating an atmosphere of teamwork. At the end of these intense periods, I'd instruct the managers to have a pizza party as a thank you, along with extra pay.

As soon as the businesses were running smoothly, Greg and I turned my mind to expansion, especially for the Hawkins battery chargers, battery load testers, electronic equipment, and welding machines. They were such high-quality products. We designed several new models specifically for worldwide markets. With our location in Durban near a busy international shipping harbor, we were perfectly poised for global distribution.

Over the next seven years, we traveled all around the globe attending trade shows. I usually took Anne and the children with me.

Our displays grew significantly from the first year in Germany when we had just eight models to show. Now, we brought twenty-five different models to international shows. We'd even constructed an innovative display which brought our booth a great deal of attention. The motorized, rotating display was seven feet tall and five feet wide, complete with mirrors and shelves. Hawkins won "Best in South Africa" display honors at several international shows.

Soon Hawkins held 65 percent of the battery charger market in South Africa and exported battery chargers to thirty other countries. Our research and development team continuously worked to innovate and maintain high quality standards. In time, Hawkins was the largest manufacturer of battery chargers in the entire continent of Africa.

We enjoyed an excellent reputation. Our contractors were making almost double what they'd earned under the old salary systems. Even though our sales increased fivefold, we didn't need to increase our workforce by more than 75 percent because of our tight focus on productivity and efficiency.

"Hey Greg, do you remember the first day we met at the old Hawkins plant?" I asked one day as we walked around the new plant.

"Sure do. I was so embarrassed at the filthy conditions and all the junk we had strewn everywhere. After we spoke, I was so eager to work with you and change things. We've come a long way."

"Yes, we have, Greg, and I could not have done it without you. You're an incredible partner, one of the few people I know who work just as hard as I do."

Few people would have seen the vast potential in the dirty junkshop of the original Hawkins factory. It was a significant risk, yet I could see the future benefits waiting there.

Businesses can show you things, like hints of greatness you must be able to read like radar. If you can see and visualize how it will look five years down the line, you can plan to realize that greatness. I was incredibly proud of that company's success, more so than almost any other, because it started in such poor conditions and grew into a global success. Over time, Hawkins became my most profitable business in Africa.

When I looked around the beautiful Springhawk complex, I felt happy and satisfied. I had four profitable companies, and delighted tenants in the other factory sites. Because I'd pushed the limits of my strength and the systems surrounding me, my dreams had all come true.

When Anne brought the children to visit me, Pany begged me to spend time in the factories, just as I had when I was a boy with my father. I felt as if I was standing on top of a mountain that had been incredibly hard to climb.

Chapter 19: A Second Taste of Danger

→

The political scene in South Africa began to change in the early 1990s. I believed the government would remain stable for a few additional years, thanks to the work of President Fredrick de Klerk and Nelson Mandela, who were working diligently to end apartheid laws which had governed South Africa since 1948. It was a complicated and volatile situation.

I admired the careful negotiations de Klerk and Mandela conducted, earning them a Nobel Peace prize. However, as apartheid ended, a massive flow of poor people moved into the cities, including Durban. The city infrastructure could not manage such a flood of people, especially since they had no housing.

Suddenly, massive tent cities sprang up all around Durban. Crime in Durban and the whole of South Africa skyrocketed. Criminals were willing to kill a person over a wallet with just fifty dollars in it. Citizens started living like prisoners behind tall walls with electrified fences. It was no longer safe to stop at a stoplight after dark. Carjackings, kidnappings, and robberies became commonplace in every neighborhood, including ours.

One night, we were away visiting friends. When we arrived home, the lights were on in the house, which was strange because it was early in the evening. "Look at that, somethings wrong. We need to be extremely careful as they might still be in the house. Anne, take the kids to the front door and stay there. Everyone, start making lots of noise."

I carefully eased open the front door and looked inside. When I could see it was clear, I said, "Okay, everyone inside. Anne, lock the door behind you so no one can follow us in. Keep making noise and stay right here in the entry. I'm going to look around."

After clearing the ground floor, I crept upstairs, noticing all the doors were open. We always kept them shut, so it was clear someone had been inside. I could hear wind blowing from the master bedroom, so I picked up a small table, shouted, and ran inside the room. The balcony door was open and the curtains blowing in the wind. I locked the balcony door, entered the bathroom to make sure no one was hiding, and then started to look around.

We'd arrived home just in time. I had a small safe cemented on the floor of the bedroom closet. When I looked at it, I could see the robbers had damaged the door to the point it was almost ready to fall open. Once I cleared all the rooms, I called for the family to come up.

We were so lucky. If we'd arrived home just fifteen minutes later, the thieves would have gotten my automatic pistol, jewelry, cash, and other valuables. They may have decided to stay behind and kill us. Our guardian angels were with us once again.

We called the police, but it took them more than an hour to arrive. They told me these kinds of robberies were happening all over our suburb and other parts of Durban, multiple times each day.

The police could do nothing to prevent them. Durban had too many desperate people willing to do anything to survive.

After we got the kids settled in bed, Anne said, "It's time to go, isn't it?"

"Yes, Sweetie, life is getting too dangerous here, just as we thought it would. It's time to put our plan in motion."

"Do you think we can wait until Nikki graduates from high school? It's just a few more years. It would make things much easier for her," Anne asked.

"I don't know. Let's start working on the details and watch things carefully here. We'll stay as long as it's safe," I answered.

I purchased a stronger safe and installed some additional security items in our home. It was hard to watch house after house in our neighborhood being robbed.

By 1992, we'd selected San Diego as an ideal location for our family and businesses. Anne and I began to envision a wonderful life there as I began to seek a business to buy so we would have an income stream in place before we moved.

On my next trip, I met a South African man, Jeff, working as a business broker in San Diego.

"Jeff, I'm looking for a very specific opportunity. It needs to be a company where I would be the majority shareholder and have a strong management team in place. I might not be able to spend much time there for a few years, so I need leaders I can trust. Finally, I'm looking for untapped potential, a company that needs improvement."

"Sure, I'll start looking around, Nick. It may take some time, but I'll find you a good opportunity," Jeff said.

After a few months, Jeff notified me he'd found a business he wanted me to see. American Lighting Supply was currently owned by two partners, Don, the senior partner, and Cliff, the minority partner. Don wanted to sell his shares of the company, while Cliff wanted to stay on. This reminded me of my partnership with Greg at Hawkins, so I became very interested.

On my first site visit, I learned American Lighting Supply (ALS) had sixteen employees working from eight garages and an office in a residential condominium. The offices looked terrible, smelly, and were filled with outdated office equipment and furniture.

ALS had two divisions, one supplying energy-efficient lighting and fixtures for commercial and government accounts and the other specializing in lighting retrofits. The retrofitting division worked in tandem with the California Public Utilities Commission and San Diego Gas and Electric. ALS was rich with potential. Even a few cosmetic changes would bring great rewards. However, I had plans beyond a nicer office.

I called Lionel, my dear CPA friend who was now in Miami, and reviewed the details with him.

"It sounds perfect for you, Nick," he said, "and, I have an idea for you. My son Steele is going to be graduating with his MBA from San Diego State this year. Why don't you hire Steele to be your eyes and ears in the company until you move? I'll help him set up all the accounting functions. Would you be willing to mentor my son in leadership and operations? I can't think of anyone better to help launch him into the business world."

I met with Steele several times and was impressed by his motivation and intelligence. This plan would be positive for everyone. Who would have thought all those many years later after that first interview with Lionel I would be working with and building an incredible business with his son on the other side of the world? It just goes to show you that you never know where one conversation can take you.

After talking things over with Anne, I purchased ALS and hired Steele. I gave him a very specific agreement with performance goals which would allow him to own a percentage of the business each year as a bonus if he met specific targets. Steele would lead the company, while Cliff managed sales. Steele and I would speak by phone each day, and I would spend at least ten days onsite each quarter.

Steele's first task was to find a new location that would provide a better company image, increase efficiency, and boost morale. I also allocated capital for new computers, software, delivery vans, office equipment, and telephone systems. We updated the employee uniforms and trained the staff to be more knowledgeable about the products and customer service. Steele and Cliff worked diligently to improve everything.

In 1993, the state of California instituted a special rebate program for large electric users such as military bases, hospitals, universities, schools, hotels, fire stations, and big commercial and government buildings. The program's goal was to replace old incandescent lighting and fixtures with more energy-efficient fluorescent lighting under this program, saving up to 80 percent in energy costs.

It was a fantastic opportunity for ALS but had one drawback. We'd have to pay for all the materials and installation, then wait for some customers to receive their state rebates before they'd pay us. We needed a great deal of capital for this kind of program. I moved more funds to the USA and prepared to take this risk, knowing it may be a tremendously profitable operation.

Thanks to Cliff's excellent sales skills and the general improvements we'd already made, ALS won some large government contracts, including a great number of US Navy buildings in San Diego. Now, I felt sure ALS business would become the foundation of my success in the United States.

During these years when I was traveling to San Diego every quarter, I took my family with me to San Diego regularly so we could become accustomed to living there. It was much easier to move a family in the 1990's than it was for my family when we left

Patras years earlier. Anne and I wanted our children to have some familiarity with the USA before we moved there so in 1993, we rented a house in La Jolla Shores, a northern San Diego suburb, for five weeks during their school break. We made a point of living not as vacationers, but as ordinary citizens.

Nikki loved San Diego from her first visit. She wanted to study aerospace engineering and set a goal to attend the University of California San Diego since it offered an excellent program.

Pany was in junior high and an avid soccer player and video gamer. He found San Diego offered him good opportunities, as well.

Athena was still quite young but was beginning to learn ice skating and showed a real talent for the sport. She'd have opportunities to pursue skating at a much higher level in the United States.

Anne and I wanted our children to have the opportunity to follow their dreams. In the United States, they could choose from a wide array of universities and career pathways.

Opportunities in South Africa were already beginning to decline. It was especially important to us that our children have opportunities. They were intelligent and hard-working, full of potential. We wanted to give them every chance at a wonderful life. Since we'd visited many areas of the United States over the years, we found San Diego to be the most pleasing because it was very similar to Durban, making the transition easier for everyone.

While Anne and I were becoming more confident San Diego would be the ideal place for us, it was heart-wrenching to consider moving from South Africa, where we were surrounded by family and friends. We'd built a beautiful life there in our dream house.

From a practical standpoint, we also had a great number of assets to sell, Springhawk, the four manufacturing companies, and my interest in the three airplanes and charter flight business. We resolved we would work hard to ensure we would not have to leave so much of our hard-earned money behind like we'd done with the Coronet Drive-In, the commercial laundry/dry cleaning business and goldmine.

Anne helped me start envisioning the perfect buyers for our properties at the ideal time. Nikki still had two years before her graduation, so we had time to do things in an orderly fashion.

I found an excellent immigration attorney to guide us through the immigration process. Because I owned a US business, I was eligible for an L-1 visa; however, it would take a long time to become citizens with that type of visa. My attorney told me about the Diversity Immigrant Visa Program (DV Program), also known as the green card lottery, in which 50,000 visas are given annually, drawn at random from the received applications. Under that program, if our names were drawn, we could receive green cards immediately and be on a short path to U.S. citizenship.

It was a gamble, of course, as it was a lottery and there was no way to predict the outcome. But we would lose nothing by trying. Since I was born in Greece and Anne in South Africa, our attorney recommended we each apply for the DV program, and we apply for the L-1, as well.

Time passed quickly and crime continued to escalate. In 1994, Anne and I decided it was time to look for a house in San Diego. It was a wise time to buy due to a depressed housing market. We contacted Linda, a real estate broker who we had met with in 1993 on our visit and had given us a wealth of valuable information about life in San Diego. From our research and from her recommendations, we decided to concentrate our search in La Jolla.

Back in Durban, I made quiet plans to begin selling my businesses.

"Greg, I want to speak with you privately. Let's go for a drive."

"I need to tell you something important, Greg. I plan to sell all my assets and move to the United States just as soon as Nikki graduates. Things here are just getting too dangerous. I love you like a brother and want to take you and your family with me. I've done the research and learned we could open a Hawkins plant in Tijuana, Mexico, just thirty miles from San Diego, where I plan to relocate. Would you be interested in moving with me?"

"Oh, Nick, I value you so much. You've taught me more about business than anyone. I'd be proud to move with you. I just don't know if my wife will agree. She is so close to her parents and siblings here," Greg replied.

"I understand, Greg. Let me give you and your family a two-week vacation in San Diego. Take your family there and see how they like it, then discuss it with your wife. All I ask is you keep this strictly confidential."

Unfortunately, Greg's wife did not want to leave South Africa. She was close to her family and could not bear to be separated. As much as Greg wanted to, his family had to come first. We felt extremely disappointed we could not continue in business together, but knew we'd always stay close friends.

Anne and I hoped we could hold out to Nikki's high school graduation, but things were becoming more intense. I worried about Anne and the kids every time they left the house. Thankfully, we had no more break-ins at our house, but Charlotte, Anne's sister, had already been robbed several times. She was now reluctant to purchase any new furniture or appliances.

Our time in South Africa had been joyous. In almost eighteen years there, we'd experienced the birth of our wonderful children, made many friends, and relished countless happy memories. I achieved many dreams there, including significant business success and learning to fly. However, all the money, success, and memories meant nothing if I could not assure my family's safety and their future.

With Anne and the children beside me, I knew we'd once again rebuild our lives and livelihood. This time though, we were going to the United States, a land of democracy and opportunity. We were sure to be safe and happy in America, a place where we could remain. All we had to do was stay safe until we could get there.

Chapter 20: Joy and Sorrow

In early 1995, a ringing telephone woke me at 4 a.m. It was my immigration attorney calling from California.

He said, "Nick, wake up your wife and jump up and down on your bed. See if you can touch the ceiling."

I had no idea what he meant. When I asked him to explain, he just repeated his instructions. Anne was awake beside me, so I told her what he said.

"Jump on our bed, you've got to be kidding."

"No, that's exactly what he said. Let's jump." We jumped on our bed, laughing in confusion.

Finally, the attorney said, "Nick, I have fantastic news. You won the DV lottery! You were selected to enter the USA with a shorter process to green cards and citizenship. You are an incredibly lucky man. All you must do is get your paperwork in order and pass an entrance interview. But there's a one catch. You won the lottery through Greece, so you and your family must complete the process at the United States Embassy in Athens."

Anne and I were overjoyed and a little daunted. Our attorney outlined the process, including collecting many pages of paperwork, traveling to Athens, and undergoing unpleasant medical tests, document reviews, and personal interviews. We had to get everything together and appear on a specific date in April. If we missed our appointment, forgot any paperwork, or failed the interviews, we would lose our opportunity. We had just a few months to prepare.

Anne went into action, dedicating herself to gathering all our documentation. It was an extremely complicated process. I had to have paperwork from Greece, Zimbabwe, and South Africa. Anne and Nikki needed documents from South Africa and Zimbabwe. Pany and Athena's files were a bit easier as they'd only lived in South Africa. I was grateful my wife was an outstanding organizer.

A few months later, we received our appointment, scheduled near the Easter holidays. That time worked in our favor. Anne and I began to make travel arrangements, first to Greece, then to San Diego. We needed to make our first official entrance in the US with our green cards. Because we always traveled during school holidays, this trip would not attract much attention from anyone in South Africa.

At that time, Nikki was seventeen, Pany thirteen, and Athena was just nine years old. Thankfully, they were all accustomed to traveling and unafraid of new environments. Our attorney coached us on precisely how to conduct ourselves during the reviews and interviews.

Anne finished our documents and stored them all in a leather attaché bag manufactured at our leather factory. She held that bag in her arms during the entire trip to Greece, never letting it out of her sight for a moment—something I believe she learned after the loss of our passports on our honeymoon. Our futures depended on the documents in that bag.

Finally, we arrived in Athens in April of 1995, checking into a newly constructed Holiday Inn within walking distance of the medical testing facility and the American Embassy so we could walk to our appointments. I felt welcomed by the familiar sights and sounds of my childhood.

However, this was not a vacation. First, we had to undergo a battery of medical tests, including screenings for HIV, tuberculosis, and other infectious diseases. After testing, we had to wait a couple of days for the results. Then, it was time to go to the Embassy for our interview. We had spent hours practicing for this interview, reviewing the paperwork, and selecting appropriate attire.

The United States Embassy in Athens was in a vast, imposing building, full of marble and soaring ceilings. I noticed it was as formal and silent as a cathedral. At that moment, I was very thankful my children were so polite and well-behaved. This was not a place for any kind of foolishness.

At every turn, it seemed as though we had to pass another hurdle. First, going through a thorough security screening at the door, then submitting our documents to a variety of gatekeepers. Finally, we were shown to a waiting room specifically for lottery applicants.

My heart was pounding. I looked at Anne and smiled, gripping her hand in encouragement and for support. We were all too intimidated to speak in a normal voice, only whispering briefly while we waited in that silent room. I'd never felt so intimidated in my life.

After what seemed like an eternity, we were ushered into an office staffed by two women. One spoke to me in Greek and the other in English. I was grateful for my skills with languages. They took our documentation and left us for about an hour, where we sat silently, waiting. I noticed I was perspiring and took a deep breath to relax.

Finally, they returned to the office. With a smile, they told us our documents were in perfect order, better than any they'd seen for a family. I turned to Anne and gave her a proud smile. Then, the women asked us all a few questions. Everyone, even little Athena, answered their questions perfectly. All our preparation was paying off.

Next, we were ushered into another office where a gentleman reviewed our medical results and documents again.

"Mr. Haritatos, what are your financial plans? How will you be supporting your family in the United States?"

"Sir, I already own a successful business in San Diego, American Lighting Supply. It is a successful venture and affords me a good income. When I move permanently, I will seek other business opportunities, as well."

That answer seemed to satisfy him as he scrutinized our bank statements and other financial documents.

"Very well. I have no further questions for you currently. I'd like you to leave here now while I continue to review your case. All of you must return in precisely two hours. At that time, we'll give you the results of your application."

As we left the building to go to lunch, we all sighed in relief. Yet, the process wasn't over so we couldn't fully relax. We thought it would be a good omen if we ordered an American meal.

Over hamburgers and fries, we discussed how we thought the process was progressing. No one finished their meal; we were all too tense. Our entire future hinged on what might happened that afternoon.

Once we returned to the embassy, we were ushered into the office of the Counsel General, the most opulent and imposing room we'd seen yet. The tension in the air was so thick it was hard to breathe.

Finally, he said, "Everything looks to be in order here. Congratulations. Please stand and raise your right hands to pledge allegiance to the United States of America."

We all stood and solemnly recited the Pledge of Allegiance, which we'd memorized in anticipation of this moment.

Then the Counsel General handed us five large, sealed manila envelopes to present to an immigration officer wherever we landed in the US and said those seven magical words: "Welcome to the United States of America."

It was such a profound moment I still tear up when I see an American flag or hear the national anthem. After getting our green cards and additional paperwork, we left the embassy in a daze. We all hugged each other tightly on the sidewalk.

We'd done it! Everything had gone according to plan. We were now free to move to the United States and leave dangerous South Africa. Anne and I had tears in our eyes as we hugged each of the children and thanked them for their outstanding performance during the long day. We'd hoped and planned for this moment for so long we felt exhilarated and full of joy.

That evening, we went out to a wonderful restaurant with some of our relatives and toasted our good fortune. We now possessed a golden opportunity—a new life in the United States of America!

We spent one additional day in Athens and then flew to the United States, landing many hours later in Los Angeles. It was different from the other times we had entered. We had to go to a particular area in Immigration and clear one final hurdle.

While we waited for the Immigration Chief Officer to review our paperwork, I remembered how it felt to enter Rhodesia so many years ago. I was about the same age then as Pany and all I could think about was seeing my father. Only now did I realize the great burden my mother endured moving all of us to a new country alone.

This was it. We were finally here. All the patience, planning, and hours of hard work all came together in this singular moment. Absolutely everything depended on this moment. We held our breath.

The chief officer asked us additional questions. Our hearts lifted as we heard again, "Welcome to the United States of America."

The process completed, we embraced and celebrated while we collected our baggage. It felt surreal. We were guaranteed entry into the United States and could apply for citizenship in five years. It was a miracle. We rented a car and drove to San Diego, exhausted from all the emotions and extended travel. I grew so sleepy on the drive Nikki and Anne talked to me and pinched me to ensure I stayed awake. At last, we arrived at our hotel. We all slept soundly, secure in the knowledge we could move to the United States.

We were so happy in San Diego and excited about our future there. We would stay for about two weeks to meet with Linda, our realtor, to look at houses. After a long search, we found a property on an immaculate estate a few blocks from the University of California, San Diego, the school Nikki wanted to attend. The design was like our beloved home in Durban, with plenty of room for family and for entertaining. It was a stunning property, with a pool, tennis court, four-car garage, eighteen beautiful palm trees, fountain, and a contemporary look. We all loved it.

Anne and I made an offer with a condition. We asked the sellers to remain in the house for up to twelve months after the sale at an exceptionally low rent so we had time to sell everything in Durban and arrange the move. I did not want to buy a beautiful home and let it sit empty or have strangers rent it while we were out of the country.

The house was so clean and well-cared for that I trusted the current owners to watch over it for us. Unfortunately, the sellers declined our offer. Linda promised to continue searching for us.

Once we returned to Durban, we felt the heavy stress of the political turmoil. We had to be extremely careful of our immediate surroundings during our final months there. We also informed our family and friends we were leaving, knowing we may not see many of them for a long time.

Every day, I bounced between excitement and sorrow. I wished the situation in South Africa, all the crime, danger, and erosion of the political systems, was not happening and we could remain in a place we'd enjoyed so much. Yet, the danger continued to mount, and it was the best choice to leave. Our family's safety was more important than anything else.

Things were hard. We all faced so many strong emotions, both excitement about our new opportunities, and sadness over leaving so much behind.

Athena was terribly worried about being separated from her best friend.

My dear friend, Henry, died from cancer.

We listed our home, but the housing market was quite depressed at the time as many professionals with comparable homes were leaving. The market was flooded. There was so much uncertainty in the country few people were willing to invest in large properties.

After three months with no serious offers, a friend of one of my pilot buddies, a South African Airways captain, offered to rent the house with an option to buy it after eighteen months. We'd hoped for a full sale, but since no other offers arrived, we drew up an agreement with the captain with the stipulation it would not go into effect until two weeks before we would move out, in case we could sell it. We let our listing contract with our realtor expire, and I paid for a large shipping container that would carry all our furniture and possessions to the US by sea.

In November, I put Hawkins on the market. I'd already found buyers for my other businesses and the Springhawk complex. We had a cash offer for the full asking price within four weeks, subject to a financial review.

My accountant, Gary, was on vacation at the time. Because I wanted to close the deal quickly, I contacted Gary and asked him to return to Durban to help me. In return, I'd buy Gary and his wife tickets to the United States and pay for a two-week vacation there as a bonus, promising him we would fly out of Durban together. Gary arrived the next day and did everything required to sell Hawkins. Greg agreed to stay with the company for at least twelve months to ensure a smooth transition. I felt so sad about leaving Greg behind.

Three weeks before we were going to move, a residential property broker I'd never met called and requested a house showing later that afternoon. The entourage arrived including the broker, a gentleman smoking a big cigar, and a bodyguard. They toured the house, asked me a few questions, and then left. The broker called later and asked if he could bring the man and his wife back the following morning.

The couple and their bodyguard arrived the next morning and carefully examined the house. It seemed strange the wife did not speak a word to me, and after they left, I could not tell if they liked the property or not.

The broker called in the afternoon and asked to meet with Anne and me the next day with an unusual offer. The couple wanted the house if they could have all the furniture and move in just ten days after buying the house. They were willing to provide a 30 percent, non-refundable cash deposit if we agreed to carry a note for up to six months. At the end of six months, the buyer would pay the balance in cash or forfeit the deposit.

I countered, saying the piano belonged to Nikki and could not stay with the house. I also asked to keep the furniture from the children's rooms. The buyer was willing to give up the piano, but nothing else. After speaking with my attorney and Henk at the bank, I realized this was the best offer we would get.

"Children, we've found a buyer for the house. There is just one change from our plan. They want all our furniture to stay here."

"I know this is a surprise and you were all planning to have your old things in our new house," Anne soothed. "Just think of how much fun we'll have picking out new furniture when we get to La Jolla.

The kids were surprised but seemed satisfied they'd be able to bring all their clothes, books, and personal items. Nikki and Athena started to talk about what kind of bedroom furniture they'd like most. As long as Pany had his computers and gaming systems, he was satisfied. I was proud of their resilient attitudes.

We signed the papers and called the shipping company to deliver the container right away. We'd already paid for a large container and could not cancel the delivery even though we had little to pack, just our clothes, books, personal possessions, the piano, and the large safe I'd purchased after the break-in.

Our movers were amazed we'd just filled the expensive container about 25 percent of capacity and looked at us like we were crazy. Then we said goodbye to our lovely house and stayed with Anne's sister for a couple of days before our departure the following Saturday.

A few days later, Peter called from Zimbabwe with terrible news. My father died unexpectedly.

In my sorrow, I realized we had to leave Durban in a few days, and the timing was going to be extremely complicated. I asked Peter if he could please plan the funeral for Wednesday so I could fly up on Tuesday, attend the ceremony, then return to Durban on Thursday. Anne and the children would not be able to come with me as there was too much to do in Durban to be ready for our departure on Saturday.

Days earlier, I'd sold my Mercedes to a friend and was driving one of his old cars. As I was headed to the Hawkins early Monday morning, a huge front-end loader turned across traffic and crashed into me. The loader pierced the windshield and took off the entire roof, pinning me in. If my guardian angel had not been watching out for me, I would have been decapitated. Right before the crash, I sensed the impact and threw myself onto the passenger seat. People at the scene pulled me out of the vehicle, saying it was a miracle I was alive. The driver hadn't seen me at all.

Between the impending move, my father's sudden death, and the car accident, I was under an incredible amount of stress as I traveled back to my boyhood home in the new Zimbabwe. It seemed ironic I would be returning there once more before I left Africa forever.

The poverty and destruction I witnessed in the former Rhodesia affirmed my decision to leave Africa. Robert Mugabe, still in power, instituted disastrous policies including nationalizing most of the food production. Peter told me the economy was near collapse.

Again, I urged Mama, Peter, and Cathreen to leave, but they were unwilling to consider starting over. Peter's government position continued to protect him and his businesses. Because of his political acumen, he'd been able to thrive under Mugabe's regime, although he always gave me credit for getting him his initial start in government.

While I was proud of Peter and Cathreen's abilities to endure the danger and corruption in the new Zimbabwe, it broke my heart to see the failing infrastructure inside the country. The former Breadbasket of Africa was now a place where people went hungry, and farms lay fallow. Unemployment was rampant.

As I stood before my father's grave, I thought of his bravery and all he'd risked leaving home to give his family better opportunities. I remembered the bakery, my businesses, and the many sweet and painful events. My father had been a continual source of inspiration and encouragement throughout my life. It was hard to imagine life without him.

Before I left for the airport the following morning, I went to my mother and hugged her tightly. I placed my face next to hers so I could look deeply into her eyes. She was aging and in poor health, so I realized this may be the last time I would be able to hug her.

"Oh, Mama, I love you so much. Thank you for all you've done for me. I will miss you so terribly."

"My sweet Nicomou, I love you with all my heart. I am so proud of everything you've done and of the beautiful family you've created. Your father was proud too. Do not worry about me. Peter and Cathreen will take care of me until I go to Heaven to be with God and your father. You are doing the right thing. You must move to America and make a good life there. May God bless you and send angels to guide and protect you always."

It felt as if my heart was shattering. I kissed her dear face once more and said my final goodbye. It was time to leave my mother and Africa behind me to ensure a good future for my children. My thirty-eight years in Africa shaped me, gave me courage, and taught me to live without limits. In just a few days, I'd follow my father's example, strengthened by my mother's blessing, and begin a new life thousands of miles away on a new continent.

Chapter 21: Welcome to America

We arrived in San Diego in early March of 1996 supported by our green cards, our hopes, and our dreams.

Steele met us at the airport with a bold proposal. He had a vision of expanding the lighting business, and it would require a significant infusion of cash—my cash.

After spending more than twenty-four hours on a plane moving my family to a new continent, I had a lot on my mind and was exhausted. Few business partners would select that moment to pitch a funding idea, but Steele did.

I had to laugh. Steele was highly motivated and reminded me of myself.

As we drove to our rental apartment, I listened to Steele's ideas, until at last I said, "Steele, I can't think about this until I read it on paper. Let me get some sleep. I will see you in the office in a day or so."

When I arrived at the office, Steele and Cliff were ready with a thorough proposal. American Lighting was selected for a large government contract which would be quite profitable, but we'd have to carry the receivables for three to six months as well as make a significant investment in inventory. Steele and Cliff proposed I invest my personal funds into the company for a few months to tide them over.

Steele and Cliff were on fire to expand American Lighting. I didn't want to put a damper on their motivation, but I didn't want to invest a large chunk of my personal wealth without a clear understanding of their plans.

I listened carefully and asked many questions. In all my business negotiations, I find listening and asking questions gives me a wealth of information. I begin with simple questions, almost 'dumb questions,' which put the other party at ease and allows me to determine if they are well prepared. Then, I move on to precise questions about every aspect of the project, especially concerning earning projections, potential risks, and timelines. When I am investing my own funds, I insist on reducing my risk in every way possible.

Steele and Cliff's plans were solid, and they'd done an excellent job of answering my questions. I could see some opportunities to restructure the strategies to maximize the company profits, get them rolling in more rapidly, and reduce my personal risk a bit.

We had several more productive meetings, and then I decided it was time to discuss the proposal with Anne. She, too, asked me questions making sure there were no holes in the plans. She knew what was most important, but she also encouraged me to dream big. With her blessing and support, I could reach for the stars. She saw the opportunities in the proposal and supported moving forward with it.

While I was considering this proposal from Steele and Cliff, Anne and I worked with our realtor Linda to find a house. Linda worked tirelessly and showed us at least twenty properties, but Anne and I could not help but compare each one to the stunning estate in La Jolla Farms we'd tried to purchase the previous year. That property became our golden standard. Everything else we looked at paled in comparison.

After three weeks of hunting for houses, and finding nothing that came close, Linda called.

"Nick, I have some news. The estate in La Jolla Farms is back on the market. The buyer couldn't finance it. The buyers are eager for a quick sale. Are you and Anne willing to pay their listing price?"

What a miracle! Anne and I readily said yes. We'd dreamed of that La Jolla Farms estate for months and could see how happy we would be living there. Linda called the listing broker, but she seemed to be stalling her, so Linda decided it was time to approach the sellers directly.

She picked us up and drove to the La Jolla Farms estate. It was still as beautiful as we'd remembered, and as we stood across the street looking at it, the owner's wife, Judy, just happened to come outside to check on the sprinkler system. Linda walked over to say hello and asked if she remembered us.

Judy was happy to see us and invited us to come in and see the house once again. As we looked around, I noticed the owners had already begun packing moving boxes. They appeared to be highly motivated to sell.

It was still immaculate. Centrally located in La Jolla Farms, the property measured well over an acre of flat land with eighteen beautiful King Palm trees and some rare, protected, and giant Torrey pines. It had a vast yard with a pool, a tennis court, a lovely gazebo, and a fishpond with a bridge and waterfall, plus a large fountain in the front with multi-colored lighting. The house was bright, modern, and open, with plenty of space for our family. It was the most stunning property we'd seen in San Diego.

Anne and I wanted that property with all our hearts. Without even stepping aside to talk it over, we offered to buy it on the spot for the full asking price. The sellers accepted it. Finally, we had our dream home. We were ecstatic.

Just eight weeks after we landed in San Diego, we moved into the La Jolla Farms estate and began making that house our home.

As I stood outside looking at the house while our things were being unloaded, I marveled. This was the house we'd dreamed of for months, now it was ours. I was standing in the United States of America, my immigration process complete, after years of waiting for just the right time to move. We'd been able to sell all our property in Durban at good prices, so we had not lost any money. And ALS was quite successful, poised for additional growth. I recalled all the stress and work that had gone into making these events happen.

In that moment, I made myself a promise. I pledged to do everything in my power to become an even greater success. Anne and my children deserved it.

Life in the United States was good. The people were friendly and welcoming, and San Diego had many former South Africans who were happy to advise us on adjusting to our new life. One of the first things we had to do was establish a credit rating by getting credit cards at department stores. I had funds in the bank but was buying things on credit from department stores. It seemed silly to finance a television set I could have easily purchased for cash, but that was how the game was played in the United States to establish credit.

The tax laws and business regulations in the United States and California proved to be much more complicated than in South Africa. Through my network, I found an excellent accountant, business broker, and attorney to guide me.

Ron, my new attorney, was a wonderful person. We began a friendship that would profoundly influence my life in the future.

Everything was falling into place. I was able to get the home we wanted and invest in expanding American Lighting. My mother's blessing seemed to give us a very smooth landing in America, coupled with all our planning and determination.

However, shortly after we moved into our house, I started to miss soccer. I'd played soccer almost all my life and loved the game deeply. Soccer is like yoga for me, profoundly relaxing. I found I could work hard all week because I played a full soccer game every weekend.

In the past, I'd never missed an opportunity to play, arranging my travel schedule to be back home in time for Saturday's game and looking for opportunities to join a game wherever I landed. I'd ask the hotel receptionist if they had a game scheduled while I was there. Many of the hotels had soccer fields where the staff played, so I'd ask to meet the team captain, then ask if I could join a game. It was a fantastic way to meet people and stay healthy. Once, I even forgot my soccer shoes and played in my dress shoes. My big toenail came off, filling my shoe with blood, but it didn't stop me from enjoying the game.

It was time to bring soccer back to my life in my new homeland.

Pany and I noticed UCSD had excellent soccer fields almost directly across the street from our home. We thought it would be fun to find about thirty people who loved soccer so we could create two teams and play each Saturday. It didn't matter if the players were students or working adults. All I wanted was players who were willing to practice seriously, listen to coaching, and have fun. We began to talk to people and generate interest.

At first, Pany and I would just go and kick the ball around on Saturday afternoons with a couple of my friends from South Africa and their sons. There were about six of us. Sometimes a few people would be playing on another field and join us.

One day, I met Jeff, a young man who was kicking the ball around with a friend of his. We invited them to join us.

Jeff loved the game but didn't know much about playing it. I began to show him some techniques. While we were talking, I learned his grandfather came from the Island of Crete in Greece. What a small world!

Jeff agreed to invite some friends, and soon there were enough players for regular soccer games every Saturday. Pany played, and I was the coach, player, captain, and organizer. The only problem was sometimes we'd get booted off the field if another group had it reserved.

Anne and I also began to invest in commercial property. At that time, the economy in California struggled, and real estate prices were low. Some of the people I consulted with advised me to stay away from commercial real estate, predicting it would be at least three to five years before the market recovered.

I did not listen to their advice. I knew the importance of the right timing in real estate. If I could purchase properties now while the market was low, I would profit if I waited for the right time. Timing is everything in real estate investing.

First, I purchased two warehouses next to each other in a big factory complex—one for ALS, the other as a rental. Later, I bought a 5.5-acre parcel of commercially zoned property in Sorrento Valley, a growing neighborhood in northern San Diego. There were few retail properties with the retail zoning available in that area. The price was far below market value with an eager seller. This deal had excellent potential.

I created an offer with a six-month due diligence period, ensuring I had plenty of time to secure permits from the city. I hired an engineer, surveyors, and an architect to draw up plans for a shopping center. In a matter of three months, some of the economic data suggested the market was bottoming out and beginning to recover. My plans were moving along nicely.

I was delighted until I received a letter from the seller's attorney. The escrow company got a similar letter. Now that land prices were beginning to go up, the seller wanted to renege on our deal. He said he'd cancel the deal unless I paid a great deal more money for the property. He even offered to pay my development expenses.

I was upset to deal with such nonsense. I'd taken the risk to purchase the property in a down market. The seller was being greedy and trying to renege on a legal sale.

I was not accustomed to people acting in such a dishonest manner. Yet, I did not want to take him to court, even though my attorney assured me I would win. Corresponding via attorneys was costly and time-consuming. Litigation would cost even more. So, I requested we all meet face to face and hammer out a solution. I insisted we solve the problem at that meeting instead of going to court.

In the end, I paid the seller more money and continued with my plans. It was more efficient to pay the additional expense then spend years and countless dollars in litigation. The delay would have been more costly than just paying the extra money and moving forward. I avoid legal battles at almost any cost because no one wins.

Back at home, everyone was settling into our new lives. Pany and Athena started at their new schools shortly after we arrived. They were both advanced one year ahead in school, just as I had been when I arrived in Rhodesia, making them the youngest students in their new classes. Nikki began her studies at UCSD in the fall. In time, the children formed new friendships, and our home became filled with laughter, art projects, dancing, and joy.

While my business success made me happy, my family gave me deep pleasure, the kind that cannot be bought and paid for.

Chapter 22: Stepping into Sunshine

In her sophomore year at UCSD, Nikki was elected co-captain of the ballroom dance team. All her years of dance lessons in Durban helped her become an outstanding dancer. One day, she learned the UCSD Athletic Department was looking for a place to host their sports clubs' awards banquet. Nikki got the idea of hosting the party in our huge garden.

I set up a meeting with Scott, the UCSD Sports Clubs director, and proposed a trade. If he would give me a permit to use one of the soccer fields each Saturday, he could host athletic banquets in the garden of my house at no cost. Scott came over to see the property and was delighted to host his banquets there.

The parties were wonderful. The university provided all the food, the band, security guards, and set-up. All we had to do was open our garden and pool to the groups of several hundred students, their coaches, and members of the administration.

We all had so much fun interacting with the students and faculty. Seeing our garden filled with happy people, eating and dancing to a live band or a DJ, brought us much joy.

One day in our second year in San Diego, I got a surprising email.

"Anne, do you remember Gary, my accountant in Durban?"

"Of course, I do. Why?"

"He has sold his business in South Africa and wants to move to San Diego! That vacation trip to San Diego we gave him and Karen must have left a lasting impression."

Anne and I invited Gary and Karen to visit us so we could discuss the pros and cons of relocating. When they arrived, we talked for hours. Gary and Karen were excited to move their two sons and daughter to the United States, so they could have more opportunities, just as I'd done. I connected them with my immigration attorney and to our beloved realtor, Linda.

Gary and his family moved to San Diego in 1998. He and Karen became dear friends—almost like younger siblings. In time, we began to discuss purchasing a business together and I tasked my business broker, Jeff, to look for potential opportunities.

At the same time, I was working on the shopping center project in Sorrento Valley. So, I'd obtained approval from the city and all the required permits for the shopping center. My architect was working on the plans.

However, about eighteen months into the project, my commercial property brokers, Brandon and Greg, came to my office with an offer on the property. Another company wanted the land. I'd already invested a great deal of money into the plans, permits, and the land, but Brandon and Greg advised me the other company was serious and would make a cash offer with a short escrow. They suggested I add up all my expenses and the land cost, then double the price.

As always, I discussed this offer with Anne.

"This sounds just like the time in Phalaborwa when we sold our land instead of building a mall. That worked out very well for us. Why don't we try it here? We can use the money to buy some commercial or office buildings."

"That is a great idea!" I replied. "It would be much easier to oversee office buildings instead of dealing with construction hassles. Sweetie, I am so lucky to have your brilliance in my life and business."

The buyers eagerly accepted my terms and purchased the property. With the money, we bought one high-end, all glass, modern office buildings in the same area, as well as two residential properties in a luxury gated community in Fairbanks Highlands, an exclusive suburb. The houses were in construction, and I knew we could sell them at a profit, which I did as market conditions improved.

When we toured one of the houses, Anne and my daughters noticed the kitchen was not very appealing. They suggested some changes to the design, which we made. As always, they had a keen eye. Once the house was finished, it was sold after one visit from a couple who loved the kitchen so much, they immediately put in an offer. I kept the other house and rented it to the developer as a fully furnished model home.

My business broker, Jeff, discovered Sunshine Rentals, a housewares company that was coming on the market.

Sunshine worked with large corporate clients who moved executives to San Diego. The clients would relocate these executives and their families into fully furnished, high-quality apartments. Sunshine provided everything for these executive apartments, including furnishings, linens, appliances, computers, even soap and cleaning supplies for one, two, or three-bedroom apartments.

Unlike some of my previous business purchases where I had to rebuild and restructure from the ground floor, Sunshine was doing well. The company had twenty employees, a fleet of trucks, and a full commercial laundry in a large warehouse. However, I could see there were opportunities to streamline operations and expand the business. Potential awaited.

Gary and I decided to purchase Sunshine together. I was the primary shareholder, as is my traditional practice, with Gary as the minority investor. My first focus was reorganizing the warehouse and inventory systems while Gary dove into the financial, sales, and billing systems. The logistics were mind-blowing at first. Some of our packages were for luxury apartments with golden striped plates and exquisite furnishings. Others were for families with children of various ages, from babies to teens. The challenge was Sunshine offered many different packages, price points, and terms. Each order had to be customized but quickly delivered and unpacked. Gary and I had much to learn.

After we streamlined operations, we increased sales substantially. Eventually, we had nearly 750 apartment units rented and another 750 units in the warehouse packaged and ready for delivery. We served customers in San Diego, Orange County, and Los Angeles. Gary and I worked very hard to master everything needed to expand Sunshine rentals.

At the same time, I was working with Steele and Cliff to grow American Lighting. Their expansion plan was successful, and the business was increasing in both its client base and profits.

Steele became like a son to me, part of the family. I was proud to mentor him to success. When he married, Anne and I hosted his wedding in our garden.

Our early years in San Diego felt golden. As the years rolled along, our ties to UCSD grew tight. Nikki and Pany attended the university, excelling academically. Anne was elected the chair of the university Parents' Council and served in that capacity for seven years. Scott and I became good friends. He brought his son to join my soccer team and would watch our games when he could.

Nikki studied aerospace engineering and competed in Latin dancing on the ballroom dance team where she became the event coordinator, organizing competitions, shows and fundraising events on campus. She had two internships for dance and marketing, and was very involved with the student organizations department, starting three new student organizations.

Pany loved video games and had an innate understanding of computers. When his high school began to install a new computer network, Pany offered to set up all the computers. The high school was so impressed by his work they contacted UCSD, who offered Pany an early admission to their Computer Science program. He played soccer and enjoyed running with me, and in time, he enrolled at UCSD, majoring in computer science and engineering. Nikki even recruited him for the ballroom dance team.

Although it took some time for Athena to adjust to life in the United States, she continued her figure skating lessons and flourished. How I loved to watch her soar across the ice! She was tiny but had incredible strength and grace. In time, she became a champion competitive ice skater who traveled worldwide, representing the United States, and winning many trophies. Her dedication to skating reminded me of my passion for business, both required discipline and dedication.

Anne and I were incredibly proud of our children. It gave us a deep joy to watch them develop into kind, loving, and successful young adults.

One year, Scott asked me to help coach the University soccer team for a few months when he was in between coaches. I was delighted! The team was struggling and discouraged by their losing record. I found many opportunities to improve the team. I changed everything, moving players to different positions more suitable for their talent, and teaching skills and good habits in training familiar in Africa and Europe where soccer was more sophisticated than in the United States.

A few of the players were unhappy with all the changes, but as the team began to win matches, everyone changed their tune. I kept the Saturday games going while I was coaching for the university twice a week. I never tired of being involved with the beautiful game of soccer, either as a player or coach.

After Scott hired a new coach, I found myself with some extra time on my hands. It was time for a new opportunity to set a goal and break some limits.

Chapter 23: A 1,200-Mile Goal

In 2000, Pany decided to do a semester at sea, sailing around the world as part of his university education. While his ship docked in South Africa, Pany took the opportunity to visit friends in Durban.

"Dad, it's Pany in Durban. Listen, I've had a lot of time to think, and I'd like to start working with you in the real estate business while I finish up my degree. Will you teach me the business?"

I was overjoyed! I'd never pressured my children into working with me, wanting each of them to find their own paths in life. When Pany asked to work with me, I felt incredible pride that he chose to learn from me. As soon as he returned to San Diego, he began working part-time with me.

At the time, I was in negotiations to buy a new, large shopping center in a prime location on the border between Vista and Carlsbad. When completed, the property would have ten buildings on ten acres, with three entrances, two drive-thru restaurants, a gas station with a convenience store, and space for many small businesses and several large anchor stores.

The current owners wanted to dissolve their partnership after completing eight of the buildings. It took some tough negotiating, but I purchased the property and began construction on the two remaining buildings.

While I was expanding my commercial real estate holdings, I also walked into an opportunity to set an incredible goal.

Back in 1998, I started hiking each Sunday with Gary and a couple of other friends, my attorney, Ron, and Phil, an artist of Greek heritage. In the last few years, we'd walked all over San Diego and the surrounding areas.

One day, in 2000, Ron started telling us about his travels in Central and Northern California when he attended university at Stanford and Berkeley in Northern California. When he was at Stanford, he'd ride his Vespa scooter to the coast whenever he needed a break. Ron told us about the California Coastal Trail (CCT), which ran along the beach and the famous California Highway 1, from Tijuana, Mexico, all the way through California, ending at the Oregon border. As we walked, Ron suggested we walk the 1,200-mile trail together.

At first, this sounded crazy. Ron was a brilliant man, but also full of jokes and wild ideas, so this was par for the course for him. However, as we walked, we began to get excited about walking the CCT. We were very near to the end of the trail at the Mexican border, so starting would be easy. I did some rough calculations in my head and told the guys it would take us about four months to walk the trail, which slightly dampened our enthusiasm. No one could get away from their responsibilities for that long.

However, I liked this idea of walking the CCT. It would be a substantial physical and mental challenge, and I wanted to think it over. I told the others I would do some research and bring the information to our walk the following Sunday. Planning the logistics required to conquer a 1,200-mile trail with a group of middle-aged men was a huge undertaking, but my mind was on a mission to solve this puzzle and create a plan to make it happen.

As soon as I arrived home, I talked with Anne. "Sweetie, Ron told me about an amazing hiking trail here, the California Coastal Trail. I think we should form a group and walk it. It's long, 1,200 miles, but we can do it. What do you think?"

"Well, that's a very long way. How would you find the time to do it? You are so busy at work."

"That's true. I was thinking we could break it into sections and do a little bit each year. I want you to come with me. You are fit and strong. Wouldn't it be fun to do this together with my walking group and their wives?"

To her credit, once again, Anne listened carefully and asked many wise questions. In our discussions, we decided if we could plan the walk carefully, we could make it fun for everyone. Anne told me she would be happy to walk the CCT with me, and if I wanted to go, she would walk beside me in full support.

Over the following days, I did extensive research on the CCT. As I learned more about the trail, my enthusiasm kept growing. The CCT project was funded by the State of California and was one of the most beautiful trails in the world. It wound along the coast, passing through cities with thriving waterfronts, farmlands, lighthouses, quaint villages, military bases, seal colonies, redwood forests, rugged mountains, and endless stretches of beach.

By the following Sunday, I had a preliminary plan to share with Phil, Ron, and Gary. We'd start at the Mexican border so we could walk against traffic and begin close to home. It would be best to walk each May, so we'd have the best weather. If we walked for eight days each year and covered ten to thirteen miles a day, we could finish the CCT in sixteen years.

"Sixteen years?" Gary asked incredulously. "That's a long time. We'll all be old when we finish."

"Oh, come on, Gary, you are the youngest one in this group." Phil laughed. "As the oldest, I say yes. It will be a grand adventure."

As we did our Sunday walk, we considered this undertaking. We'd have to think about things like restroom access, navigating in remote areas, walking in rain and fog, food, transportation, and how to include enough fun so our wives would want to join in. The guys asked me to do all the planning and logistics because they knew I would enjoy it and devote all my energy to creating a well-considered plan for the journey.

I discovered a two-volume set of books covering the CCT in detail, *Hiking the California Coastal Trail* by Bob Lorentzen and Richard Nichols, who walked the trail from Oregon to Mexico. I took copious notes and filled the books with sticky notes and highlights.

I called on all my logistical skills to plan this incredible journey, recalling my days preparing patrols at the protected villages in Rhodesia and all my pilot training. I had to consider everything—safety, weather, highway and parking access, varying fitness levels, clothing, and equipment, lodging and food, transportation, and communications.

While I worked on dividing the 1,200-mile trail into eight-day segments and all the other areas of consideration, Anne started talking with the other wives to get them excited about the trail. The women were all friends of Anne's and trusted her, so she was the ideal person to present them with the idea. The guys in the walking group got an update each week. We decided to invite a few other friends so our group would consist of twelve to fourteen people.

Everyone in the group was thrilled to take on such a glorious goal. Walking the CCT from end to end would be an adventure few others achieved. We all had a history of personal and professional accomplishments, but the CCT would crown them all. It was almost impossible to imagine undertaking a quest to cover 1,200 miles over the course of many years, but we were invigorated and ready for the challenge.

It took me more than six months to plan the trip. I planned for us to rent two passenger vans to carry the walkers and our equipment. Each person would be able to bring a suitcase and backpack. I developed lists of the shoes, clothing, snacks, and first aid supplies each person would need, studying the best kinds of hiking boots and the right socks for walking on paved trails, sand, and rough mountain terrain. I studied maps to locate parking lots where the vans could meet us for breaks, re-supply, and help in case of injury or exhaustion. We would need walkie talkies, compasses, and accurate maps.

I also considered what we'd do when we were not walking. It would be fun to visit some of the Spanish Missions along the trail and go canoeing or jet boat cruising down some of the big rivers when possible. Anytime we would have the opportunity to go dancing, visit a local festival or hear live music, we'd do it. While this was a serious walk, it had to be fun too.

Anne and I had hosted several orientation meetings with the group, providing a detailed itinerary for the eight-day walk along with packing lists of everything people would require. Everyone knew about the proper shoes, socks, clothing, and equipment they'd need to walk ninety miles over the eight days.

Finally, the day arrived to begin our long journey in May of 2001. Ron and Yvonne, Phil and Gloria, Gary and Karen, Anne's sister Oonagh and her husband Steve, and Ron's sister Joanna joined Anne and me as we walked the first steps of the CCT. Our first hike was easy. We just drove to the southern part of San Diego county and started walking on the CCT, which lay on wide, sandy beaches. Every day we'd walk on the beach surrounded by the sea, parks, playgrounds, and beautiful homes.

We continued to walk through San Diego County the following year. The trip became more complicated in May of 2003 when we left San Diego County. Our goal that year was to make it all the way to Alamitos Bay near Los Angeles, the first time we'd stay in hotels during our trip.

I would brief the group every morning at seven as we began the trail, telling them what time we'd meet the van for breaks, the location of restrooms and picnic tables, and reviewing the course we'd cover that day. I was so happy to see the way each day unfolded smoothly. I will never forget the scent of the sea mixed with the wildflowers blooming as we walked that section of the trail. It seemed as if we were walking in the Garden of Eden.

However, things changed when we arrived at Crystal Cove Beach at three-thirty in the afternoon of our third day. The tide reports said the tides would start to come in about that time, covering the sand. The beach had large boulders in front of steep cliffs. I gathered the group and told them I was concerned we'd be trapped by the high tides with no way off the beach except to scale the rocks and cliffs.

I recommended we go back about 500 yards, cut through a residential complex, and walk along Highway 1 for three miles to where our vans were waiting.

"I don't want to waste time going backwards," Ron said. "I'm not afraid of the tide, I've been swimming in it all my life. I'm going forward."

Steve agreed. "Me too. I'm fast and should be able to beat the tide. If not, I'll climb the cliffs. The rest of you can do what you want, but I'm going ahead."

"I don't think this is a good idea. However, if you two want to try it, it's up to you. I'm going to take the safest route. Who's coming with me?" I replied.

I took the rest of the group back along the trail while Steve and Ron set off along the beach. It took us about fifty minutes to go through the residential complex and reach an area along the highway to see the beach. We couldn't see anyone there. We waited a few minutes and tried to call Steve and Ron, but we didn't get an answer. Hoping they were in front of us, we continued walking to the vans.

We reached the vans about 5 p.m. There was no sign of Steve or Ron. We drove to a nearby ranger station and informed them about the situation. They came with us back to the trail to see the area where Steve and Ron should have been walking.

The rangers said, "Those cliffs are impassable at high tide. We have warning signs posted about the danger."

At 5:45 p.m., the rangers suggested we drive to a hill to look over the beach. If there were no signs of Steve and Ron, they would call 911 and alert the search and rescue teams.

As we drove back, we saw two people walking on the highway—it was Steve and Ron. We were thrilled to see them, but it was clear they were injured. They were both bloody. Ron looked terrible, soaking wet, blue with cold, and shaking. We quickly alerted the rangers to call off the search and returned to our hotel.

Everyone was quiet and shaken. It had been a very scary afternoon. Ron did not come down for dinner that night.

While we ate, Steve told us of their harrowing experience. When they reached the rocks at Abalone Point, the water was already almost up to their knees. Rather than turn back, they continued while the tides grew deeper. The waves began crashing against the rocks violently. Finally, they realized they would have to scale the rocks and cliffs, but the climb was too difficult for Ron, so he dove off the rocks into the sea, intending to swim to safety.

Thankfully, Ron was a very experienced, strong swimmer. He let the current carry him far out to sea and slowly began to make his way past the point to the beach. However, he was bruised and battered as the powerful tides bashed him against the rocks, but after a long while, he made it to the shore and struggled onto the sand. He'd lost his phone and was injured, but glad to be alive. A less powerful swimmer would have drowned.

As Ron was struggling in the water below, Steve was climbing the cliffs, scraping his hands on the rocks as he tried to find stability and a pathway. Eventually, he did reach the cliff top, and he walked the shore until he found Ron and helped him get to the highway.

The next morning, I met with Ron and Steve before the hike.

"Look guys, yesterday was almost a tragedy for you two. You might have been killed. I'm responsible for this trip and want everyone to have fun, not worry. If you want to keep walking with us, I'll need your word you'll stick with the group. Are you willing to do that?"

They agreed. Ron was not able to walk for the rest of the trip and had to ride in the van, which embarrassed him enough I imagined he'd be more cautious in the future.

Thankfully, the remaining days of this trip were easy. We walked primarily on wide, beautiful beaches in perfect weather. Everyone was happy and eager to undertake the next leg of the CCT the following May.

However, when I returned home, I realized even more acutely I carried a heavy burden. The lives of my walkers were in my hands. I was responsible for their safety. The incident with Steve and Ron taught me even wise friends could make foolish choices leading to tragedy. I had to find a way to ensure each walker understood potential dangers along the trail and would accept my leadership.

There was much to consider before the next trip. If we were going to meet our goal of walking the 1,200-mile trail, I had to work harder. As soon as I returned home, I began planning the 2004 leg of the journey.

Chapter 24: All in the Family

The summer after Pany graduated from UCSD in 2003, he started creating a video game development company, a goal he'd established as a boy. However, he had more on his mind.

"Dad, I'd like to become your partner in the real estate business. I like the work and am ready to learn more. I'd like to take the real estate broker's license exam so I can broker our deals in the future. I want you to teach me about the rest of the business."

I was delighted to bring Pany into my business, but I had one crucial question: "Son, how are you going to run two businesses at once? You will have both your game development business and this real estate business on your shoulders. It will be a great responsibility for such a young man."

Pany replied, "Dad, I am your son, with your genes. You had multiple businesses when you were this age. You worked long hours and made sure everything ran smoothly. I will do the same. And I know you won't leave me. You'll be there to help me with any problems. It's time for you to slow down and enjoy your life more."

Pany made me very proud that day. He studied hard and then passed all the real estate exams successfully, becoming a property broker. I put him in charge of managing the team leasing our two shopping centers. We worked together on the loans to construct the two new buildings, manage the construction contracts, and all the new leasing agreements. It was a big job.

In February 2003, Nikki asked to join us in the property management company. Nikki's skills with finance and her engineering systems thinking provided an excellent contribution to our family team. We all worked from home.

Over time, the company grew beyond the capacity of our home offices, so I decided we needed an impressive office that would provide a beautiful working environment and a place where we could welcome visitors for meetings. We found a fantastic office located in La Jolla Shores, just three miles from our home.

Later that year, Steele asked to meet with me at American Lighting Supply. The company was doing fantastic work. The company was bustling with jobs in San Diego County under the state grants, retrofitting many large commercial and government buildings. We also had a wholesale division supplying equipment and electrical components to the companies we retrofitted as well as some retailers.

ALS started as a sixteen-person company working out of garages and an old apartment. Now, we had more than eighty staff working in the retrofit division, and another twenty in the office, sales, warehouse, and wholesale division.

ALS had done such a great job retrofitting some of the buildings at the Navy base in San Diego the Navy asked us to do a similar project on Bremerton Navy base in Washington State. That project was colossal, requiring about twenty people working there for at least two years.

I was delighted by the growth Steele and Cliff built over the years at ALS. However, when I met with Steele that day, he looked drawn and tired.

He told me when he'd tried to hug his young son, his son was frightened and pulled away. Steele was working sixty-hour weeks managing all the growth, and his family was suffering. He knew he'd been working too much. However, until his son pulled away from his embrace, he did not realize he was harming his family.

Steele was like a son to me. I never wanted him or his lovely family to suffer because of his responsibilities. We tried hiring assistants and shuffling some of his duties, but Steele still felt burdened and burned out, so Steele, Cliff, and I eventually concluded it was time to sell the company. We were proud of what we'd built together. Now it was time to let it go.

During that time, I thought deeply about my next steps. The climate for manufacturing in the United States was challenging as many factories were moving to Mexico and other countries. I'd looked for a long time for a manufacturing business in San Diego and couldn't find any that suited my skills.

When I discussed my thoughts with Anne, we decided to shift our focus to just commercial real estate. It would be much easier for Pany and Nikki to deal with tenants instead of all the complexities of manufacturing.

Around that same time, Gary and I decided to sell Sunshine Rentals. We'd improved and expanded the business, and it was time to sell. As always, when I felt I'd improved a business as much as I could, I liked to sell it and uncover a new challenge.

In time, I purchased an additional office building and two shopping centers in outlying areas of San Diego. As our company grew larger, we added two additional assistants.

Athena, now a high school student, also began to work part-time in the office with us. Pany handled all the tenant-facing work, Nikki managed the finances, permits, contracts, and property aesthetics, and Athena helped with filing and assisting wherever needed.

I loved having all my children working with me. It was a joy to teach my children all I'd learned about business and see them grow into their roles within the company. When Athena completed her degree in environmental studies from the University of San Diego, she joined the family business full-time, excelling in daily operations. She was an organizational genius, much like her brilliant mother.

My children were so much like me, but they also had Anne's creativity and wisdom. While they were working in the family business, they all had other businesses at the same time. Pany continued to grow his game development company. Nikki had a dance company and produced events, and Athena opened a custom cake business.

We had such a good time working together. Each of them found a specific role in the company and fulfilled it successfully. Not many siblings can work together so smoothly, but my three children have always been close with each other. Their strong bond enabled them to run the property business effectively and profitably.

As my business responsibilities lessened, I found I had more time on my hands, so Anne and I began to travel extensively. I also had the opportunity to devote more time to my soccer games as well as organizing the annual CCT walks.

In 2004, we walked the section from Seal Beach to Malibu, passing over the border between Los Angeles and Ventura Counties.

One day, we stopped by the Ventura Harbor for a late lunch. I noticed a nice-looking Greek restaurant near the marina and asked the group if they'd like to dine there. Everyone agreed wholeheartedly.

I was immediately impressed with the restaurant, which was clean, spacious, and featured friendly staff. After we finished our delicious meals, I asked the staff if the owner was present, and I asked her to invite him to speak with me when he had time.

When the owner arrived, he introduced himself as Gerry. He was from the island of Kefalonia, just like my ancestors. We struck up a lively conversation. Gerry knew my friend from Durban, Gerry K, my uncle, Constantinos, and my cousin, Maki.

"Gerry, this is Nick in San Diego. How are you? Hey, I met a friend of yours from Ventura, Gerry, the one with the Greek restaurant."

When I called Gerry K. in Durban and told him about meeting the other Gerry, we laughed at what a small world it was. I'd met Gerry years ago when I had my laundry and dry-cleaning business in Durban. Gerry owned a competing commercial laundry and started hearing about this other Greek guy in town, so he came to see me. That meeting was the beginning of a great friendship.

Gerry was from the Island of Kefalonia and owned a ship chandlering business where he supplied the large cargo ships coming into Durban's harbor, along with his large laundry. Of course, he knew my Uncle Constantinos and cousin Maki. We had a lot in common as we both liked sports, business, and our shared Greek ancestry. Gerry made a trip to visit me in San Diego in 1998, which was a wonderful reunion.

I called Gerry to tell him I was returning to Durban for a visit. We'd been gone for nearly ten years. Anne's siblings had invited us to return for a big family reunion. I felt reluctant to return to South Africa as I dreaded seeing how the business environment had deteriorated. However, it was time to go back and see the family.

I also had a plan in mind for Gerry. I wanted to organize a four-day walk from South Durban to North Durban for all my friends. Gerry said yes right away, as did Henk, Stavros, Doug, and some of my other friends from my time in business and flying.

This walk would be less strenuous than the CCT hikes. We'd stop and eat in restaurants along the way as we walked along the stunning coastline. I could not wait to see my friends and introduce them to trail walking, so I got busy planning the trip.

When Anne, the kids, and I stepped off the plane in the Durban airport, more than forty people were there to greet us—family members, former neighbors, and friends. It was a beautiful surprise. We all hugged and celebrated by going to lunch at the restaurant in the airport. Our group was so large we took up more than half of the tables. I'll never forget how we all talked and laughed, reconnecting after a decade.

We had a wonderful time at the family reunion. Anne's siblings rented a big house right on the Indian Ocean in a very remote area called the Wild Coast, about a five-hour drive south of Durban. For four days, thirty of us crowded together in that big house, sharing meals, soccer games on the beach, and lots of conversation.

After the reunion, we stayed with Anne's sister, Charlotte, in Durban. She'd been robbed so many times she had little left in her home, no television and no beds, just mattresses on the floor. Charlotte refused to keep buying new furnishings just so they could be stolen.

It was heartbreaking to see how the increased crime had impacted her. I was so glad I'd gotten my family out of South Africa and talked with Charlotte about her exit options.

Over the next four days, I met my friends each morning for our walking tour of Durban. It was nice to see the improvements on the waterfront, and over the four days, we had plenty of time to share stories from our past adventures and the events we'd experienced separately over the last ten years. We never ran out of things to discuss.

It was strange to be back in Durban. We walked near the Virginia Airport, where I flew my planes, and other familiar places, but I could not bring myself to visit our old house or the Springhawk complex.

The guys asked me many questions about the United States and my life in San Diego. After telling them about my business experiences, I shared my current goal of walking the CCT.

They were astounded. As we walked and talked, I shared how I organized each annual walk. The guys were curious about all the logistics and the adventures we had along the trail.

Out of the blue, Gerry said, "We should all walk the Island of Kefalonia together. As far as I know, no one has ever walked the entire perimeter of the island in a circle before. Most people cut through the center areas. Nick, you are fit and energetic and used to hiking along the California Coastal Trail. This will be fun!"

Once I heard no one else had hiked around the entire island of Kefalonia before, I was very excited to try it. That hike would be a wonderful challenge to plan and execute. Plus, it would help me share my Greek history with my friends from Africa and America. I couldn't wait to share the idea with Anne to see if she wanted to make the trip. I wanted her by my side, as she'd been for most of my life.

The more we discussed this idea, the more excited we became. We started to imagine the trip together. We talked about the challenges of planning the trip since none of us lived in Greece.

At first, it seemed like a joke, but soon, the trip seemed possible. Gerry owned a hotel on Kefalonia, traveled there regularly, and knew many people. I had my cousin Maki and other relatives there who might also be willing to help.

We decided to schedule the walk for October of 2005. Gerry volunteered to handle all the lodging and meals if I would plan the other logistics. I asked all the Durban walkers if they'd like to participate, and soon, Gerry, Henk, Doug, and Stavros all committed to joining the adventure. I told them to take some dance lessons because we would dance like Zorba the Greek on Kefalonia. They knew me well enough to know I wasn't kidding.

I believed some of my San Diego friends would also want to join the group. We'd have a Durban and a San Diego contingent and walk around the island where my ancestors lived. I could have never imagined such a trip. I could hardly wait to begin planning it.

I'd always believed I controlled my own destiny. This 120-mile trip around Kefalonia seemed like destiny, a perfect opportunity to come full circle, back to Greece where my life began. Once I learned of this opportunity, I had to make it happen.

Chapter 25: In the Steps of Odysseus

When I returned to San Diego, I contacted my cousin Maki and told him about our plans.

"That sounds amazing, Nick. I've never heard of anyone walking around the island. It's very steep in some places, but if anyone can make that trip, it's you. I'll be glad to help! Did you know I'm a mayor now?"

"Wow, Maki, you are an important guy. Tell me more about it."

"I'm the mayor of Sami. I have an idea. Nick, I want you to begin and end your journey in Sami. I'll arrange a ceremony with the town's municipal band. They will play music to welcome you and help you begin your walk. I'll walk with you as you leave Sami. Then, the band, my wife, and I will meet you at the end of your trip and bring you back to Sami with a big celebration."

His idea sounded perfect.

Next, I called Peter and invited him and his wife Angela to join us. Unfortunately, Peter was not able to get away from his duties for that long. He was still working in the government, running the bakery, a gold mine, various businesses, and his large ranch. Peter worked in a variety of high-level positions for twenty-four years, rising to the highest ranks in Zimbabwe national affairs thanks to Robert Mugabe mistaking him for me all those years ago.

When we returned to San Diego, I started to create a strategy for motivating some of my walking group to join the Kefalonia Island walk. Ron and Yvonne were the first to say yes. Soon, Gary and Karen agreed to come along.

I was hoping Phil and his wife Gloria would join us because they were very physically fit and would be able to manage the challenging parts of the walk. Plus, Phil's parents were from Sparta and taught him much about his Greek heritage. He'd never had the opportunity to visit Greece.

I set up the trip to incorporate two weeks of extra exploring in Greece, including Athens, Sparta, Delphi, Olympia, Patras, and several other cities. Anne and I hired a Greek dancing instructor to come to our house for a set of ten group dancing lessons, so everyone was ready to have fun together and dance along our Greek journey.

Kefalonia is the largest island on the west side of Greece facing the Ionian Sea. Our walking trip would cover 120 miles along beaches, steep cliffs, and mountains. Parts of it would be quite challenging over rough terrain.

I spent months planning both the next section of the CCT walk in May of 2005 and the Greek walk the following October, plus the extra two weeks of touring around Greece for the San Diego contingent.

Planning a trip like this for people from two different continents on a third continent was extremely complicated. I was glad Gerry and Maki were handling the hotels and restaurants for me. Gerry sent me a large map of Kefalonia, which was very helpful.

I also contacted my cousin Nikos in Patras, the boy I had all those adventures with riding in my little silver car and asked him if he'd like to join us. Nikos had become a professor of Economics and was now the chief of the tax bureau in Patras. He could not walk with us but provided many useful suggestions. He invited us to come and visit him in Patras, promising a tour of the city.

I arranged to rent two vans for our trip and plotted out our daily walks so Gerry and Maki could set up the hotels. Additionally, I reserved the top floor of a hotel in Athens' Constitution Square, with lovely balconies overlooking the Parthenon and the Acropolis for our first three nights together.

My Greek heritage had always been very important to me. It was thrilling to take my dear friends to the country of my birth and share its history and culture. I wanted to ensure everything was perfect on this journey so my guests would always remember the glory of Greece.

All the plans were coming together nicely until I got a call from Gerry's wife, Yota. Gerry had died. He'd had a massive heart attack and passed the day before in Durban.

I could barely catch my breath. Gerry was a runner and an extremely healthy person. I could not believe he was gone.

"Oh, Yota, I am so sorry! What a terrible shock."

"Yes, I still can't believe it, Nick. I must tell you; Gerry was so excited about walking Kefalonia with you. He'd already contacted many people on the island who offered to help and even walk with the group for a while. There is something strange. He told me several times that if anything ever happened to him, he wanted me to help you with the walk."

Yota began to cry. In a few moments, she continued, "Nick, this trip was so important to Gerry. Please let me finish the arrangements. I promised Gerry and want to keep my word. In fact, I am moving back there. Gerry wanted to be buried on the island so

I'm taking him home and going to live there. I'll see you on Kefalonia, and Gerry will walk with you in spirit."

Losing Gerry devastated me. I wanted to find a way to honor him, so I asked Phil, who was a graphic artist, to design an acrylic plaque in honor of Gerry and our walk. We'd carry that plaque with us and place it on his grave during our walk.

After months of planning, we all arrived in Athens. I loved introducing the two groups of my friends to each other, both people from South Africa who'd known me for many years and my friends from San Diego.

We spent the first three days in Athens, walking together and exploring the ancient city. Everyone got along well. Anne and I were delighted and anticipated a beautiful adventure.

One of the highlights of our time in Athens was a soccer match with two very special escorts. There were two men who'd been part of my team in San Diego while they were graduate students at UCSD who'd returned to Greece after graduation. When I wrote to them to tell them about our trip, they offered to take us to an important professional soccer match in Athens. It was thrilling to watch soccer with my old friends in the new Olympic stadium with sixty thousand screaming spectators.

After touring Athens for a few days, we drove across Greece towards the coast, stopping to see the sights. When I took everyone to the ancient Olympic stadium in Olympia, I remembered running around it with my father and later with Anne. My heart and mind were filled with warm memories with every step. It was wonderful to be back in Greece.

When we arrived in Sami, Maki, Yota, her family, and other friends were waiting to welcome us. After settling into our hotel, we swam, enjoying the ocean and beautiful beach. That evening we had a lovely dinner with Maki and his wife, Betsi, who thanked me for the beautiful leather coat I'd made for her years ago at my leather factory in Durban. She still wore it!

The next morning, we had a special ceremony outside our hotel. As promised, Maki arranged for the small municipal band to play music and introduced our group and journey around the island. A small crowd gathered to listen.

People had many questions, so I spoke in Greek and briefly talked about my family roots on the island, life in Patras, the trip to Rhodesia and South Africa, and that I now lived in the United States. I gave profuse thanks to Maki and Yota for all their help and invited any of the villagers to walk with us as long as they wished. Once the band began to play again, Anne and I danced in great joy, joined by the others in our group.

After our dancing, we began our journey. Maki and Betsi, Yota, and some of their friends walked with us for the first hour or so. As they turned back to Sami, we promised to meet them in Argostoli for dinner and dancing on the following Saturday evening. They wished us a safe journey as we began to climb the first of many steep hills.

I carried a boom box on my back and played Greek and American music all along the way. The San Diego contingent wore pins on their hats with American and Greek flags. Everyone from Durban sported flag pins from South Africa and Greece. The energy and excitement in our group made me feel like I was floating above the ground.

The island was stunningly beautiful. We walked on narrow roads past tiny villages, thriving towns, rural lands, and beautiful beaches. The local people were curious about us. They would come out to meet us from the villages and walk with us a bit. Farmers would give us grapes cut right off the vine or a sampling of their succulent tomatoes. We saw Haritatos Hill and Haritatos Avenue, named in honor of some of my ancestors.

The eleven-day walk was quite challenging because there were so many mountains to climb. Phil, Anne, and I were the only ones able to manage it all without taking rest breaks in the van. How blessed I was to have such a strong woman by my side.

The Greek expatriate community is strong everywhere around the world. During our walk, I met people my father knew in Rhodesia, some who'd fled the Congo and came to my father for help, friends of mine from Gatooma and Fort Victoria, and many Greeks I knew in Durban. I'd call them as we came near their villages, and they would meet us. We had many beautiful lunches and dinners hosted by people from my past. It was as if I was reliving my entire life during that walk. My heart was full.

When we got to the capital city of Argostoli on Saturday, we relaxed and prepared for a two-night stay at Gerry's hotel, set in a beautiful location beside the harbor. Gerry's brother managed the hotel and welcomed us warmly.

That evening we met Yota, Maki, and Betsi for dinner and dancing at the hotel as promised. It was a wonderful experience to dance with my friends from Greece, Africa, and America. All our dance lessons paid off, and we had a wonderful time dancing and celebrating.

The following day, we walked an eight-mile section of the trail in the morning and then went to Yota's house for a delicious lunch. After the meal, we presented her with the plaque we'd made in Gerry's honor. We drove to his family village of Kardakata to visit his grave. Gerry's mother, Yota, and his daughters joined us at the graveside.

I could not contain my tears. It seemed so cruel Gerry was taken from us so suddenly. I remembered all the times we flew together, ran marathons, and spent time with our families. Anne held me close, reminding me she was with me and I should never forget her love for me. It was a painful afternoon as I mourned the loss of my good friend.

On the next day, we paused for a bit at the bay in Angonas. This village was very important to me because many people believe it was Odysseus's birthplace. I could see the island of Ithaca across the water, the city memorialized in books and poems about Odysseus. I sat by the water and thought about Odysseus's journey thousands of years ago. I'd journeyed far from my home as well, in search of adventure and success. He'd always been a hero to me, and now I walked along the same land, recalling all the places I'd traveled.

The eleventh day marked our return to Sami. Maki and some of his friends, along with the small band, met us and escorted us back into town. We had triumphed, and that night we hosted a nice dinner for Maki, Betsi, and Yota. Everyone from the walking group was happy and thanked us all for the remarkable experience.

Early the following morning, we took the ferry to Patras. Nikos was waiting for us. I grabbed him in a hug and held him tightly. I was so happy to see my childhood friend and dear cousin after what seemed like a lifetime apart.

Nikos served as our navigator and guided us all over Patras for the next two days. He rode in the passenger seat of the lead van, directing me on where to drive, and gave us a history of the city as we drove.

The Castle of Patras, a fortress constructed in the sixth century and the treasure of the city, was the highlight of the tour. The castle sits high on a hill and overlooks the entire city and the harbor. It was hard to believe I was standing there with friends from Africa and America, as well as my dear cousin, gazing down upon the landscape of my childhood. Nikos pointed out our neighborhood school, the soccer field, the bakery building, and the church where I was baptized.

As I looked over Patras, my mind flooded with beautiful memories of my parents, friends, and early years. Nikos and I told a few funny stories about our adventures in my little silver car. It was a surreal moment, smelling the scents of my childhood, seeing the places where I'd lived and played, and remembering my past. It almost felt as if my ancestors were with me at that moment.

I've always been proud of my Greek heritage. While I knew I would not return to live in Greece, I honored the strength, intelligence, and courage of those Greek ancestors, especially those who traveled the world to seek their fortunes.

We spent the next two days touring with Nikos. He took us on a walking tour of our old neighborhood where I saw familiar streets and the bakery where my father encountered the Nazis and baked bread that fed our family and many others.

On our final day, we walked across the Harilaos Trikoupis Bridge, which is one of the longest suspension bridges in the world. The bridge was constructed in 2004 in preparation for the Olympic games in Greece.

That day was special because it was the anniversary of the day when Greece refused to capitulate to Italy and Germany sixty-five years earlier in 1940, pledging to fight for independence instead of passively accepting occupation. As we walked over the 1.8-mile bridge, I thought about how this trip was bridging all three parts of my past together.

In the evening, we went for dinner with Nikos and his wife, enjoying fabulous food and more dancing. It was our final night together as a group. On the following morning, the Durban group went on their way, and Anne and I took the San Diego group on our two-week tour around the rest of Greece.

When we returned home, I was happy and relieved. All my meticulous planning paid off. The trip worked out beautifully. No one was injured, we did not get lost, and we experienced no serious problems. We'd walked over rugged terrain, drove many miles across Greece, and had many beautiful experiences. I'd also met friends and relatives I'd not seen for decades, including my 97-year-old Uncle Constantinos, who was still riding his bike!

It was a beautiful homecoming and reconnection with my past. I still mourned Gerry but felt he looked out for us all along the journey. Yet, I was glad to return to San Diego where Anne and I built a life that suited us perfectly.

I had no regrets. Instead, I was excited to see what adventures were coming next. I had things I still wanted to do and plans I wanted to make as life continued to propel me into the future.

Chapter 26: Heading North

The following ten years passed by swiftly. I had no worries about having to move my family and my business to another country. We were safe and happy in San Diego. I was a grateful man.

Anne and I relished seeing our children thrive. Pany married a wonderful woman, Cheryl, who we loved dearly. His video game design company became extremely successful and was acquired by a large corporation. They made Pany an offer he could not refuse to join their organization, so he and his family moved to San Francisco in 2009, where he later became an internationally recognized expert in game development design while operating a few other businesses of his own at the same time.

Nikki and Athena took over our family business. They did an admirable job, even during the challenging years following the real estate turndown. I enjoyed working with my daughters and watching them grow into powerful businesswomen.

In time, they also decided to pursue their own opportunities. Nikki moved to Texas and became a consultant and creativity coach. Athena started an environmentally friendly live Christmas tree business and took an executive position in one of Pany's companies.

I brought in property managers to take over daily operations. My role was buying and selling properties as opportunities came along. Anne and I did a great deal of traveling.

One year, we joined Ron and a few other friends in a seven-day walk around Manhattan Island in New York. It was fascinating to walk in an urban area, covering the entire island. Instead of sandy beaches on the CCT, we walked past Wall Street, the United Nations, universities, Central Park, Harlem, and other fascinating sections of one of the most populated islands in the world. We started and ended our journey on Wall Street, a fitting location for someone who loves business as much as I do.

My creative focus centered on the California Coastal Trail walks. We'd made a lot of progress since we began our annual walks in 2001. Over the years, we'd completed the entire southern section of the CCT, covering 600 miles of the trail. I turned to the next volume of the guidebooks by Bob Lorentzen and Richard Nichols, covering the trail's northern section.

Planning and logistics became complex as we moved further north along the trail. Now, I had to factor in travel time at the beginning and end of each walk, and in time, we had to fly the group to Oakland to begin our walks as it became too far of a drive from San Diego. The northern section of the trail is also more mountainous and remote, so it was more physically demanding.

Our group changed a bit from year to year. We continued our tradition of walking during the day and staying in a hotel every evening. There was always time for fun and dancing at least once during every trip. One by one, we walked through all of California's famous coastal cities. However, the main attraction was the incredible beauty of the land, sea, and sky.

As we progressed northward, we passed through vast farmlands, forests filled with ferns and towering trees, rocky cliffs, and breathtaking beaches. We saw thousands of birds, seals, whales, dolphins, and sea lions and walked through areas frequented by bears and mountain lions. There were military bases, lighthouses, fishing villages, and beautiful communities. Every day was different and required I lead our group with an eye for their safety, health, and enjoyment.

We encountered a problem near San Simeon. The trail went over the beach and then led up treacherous cliffs. Some of the ladies in our group could not manage the steep climb and didn't want to make the long walk back to our starting point. We all joked they might just have to live on that beach. However, I always had strong ropes and gloves on the trail, so we put them to good use that day.

I took a few of the men up the cliffs with the ropes. Then we pulled and boosted the women up the cliffs one at a time, with a man behind her to break her fall in case of a slip. Everyone worked together.

I was proud no one panicked, and we could pull together to overcome the obstacle before the high tides created a dangerous situation. Instead of a frightening experience, it was an exciting one.

The coast grew wilder as we moved northward. There were sections where we'd have to walk along Highway 1 because the beach was too rocky or the cliffs too treacherous. In some remote areas, I had to rely on my old tracking skills from my military service when the trail would disappear for a bit, or we'd come to a fork without any signs telling us which way to proceed. The weather grew cooler and rainier, as well. We encountered unexpected challenges but found ways to overcome each of them.

The year we walked north of Monterrey, we had to cross the Salinas River as it merged with the ocean. This was a dangerous section of the trail as it wound along the beach on very soft sand, making walking difficult. We'd have to cross the river on foot, which was quite dangerous during high tides.

The day we were to cross the Salinas was cold. We were walking on an open beach in a very isolated area facing a strong wind, and it was impossible to walk fast under those conditions. Based on the tide charts, I learned the tides at the river would be lowest at 2:25 in the afternoon, giving us a safe window until 2:45 when they would turn high and dangerous. Before we reached the river, we had to cover at least five miles of a deserted beach.

I was worried about Ron. He wasn't feeling well and struggled to keep up with the group during the previous days' walks.

"Ron, I've got an idea. Why don't you ride in the van until we cross the river? It's going to be cold and wet crossing. You can catch up with us on the north side and then keep walking."

"Thanks, Nick, but I don't need to ride in the van. I don't want to miss crossing the Salinas River. It's famous. You don't have to worry about me. I'll keep up with the group. Let's go."

As we walked on the soft sand, the sun disappeared. The sky filled with dark clouds, and a strong wind coming from the water buffeted us, making it exceedingly difficult. In time, Ron fell back from the rest of the group, eventually to the point where we could not see him. We decided we'd go forward towards the Salinas and scout for the best place to cross it, hoping Ron would catch up with us there.

We arrived at the river at 2:35, just a few minutes before the tide would turn. The waves on the beach were already pounding the surf and spreading white horses of sea water into the river. There was no time to delay if we were going to cross, so we walked up the river to some calmer water.

"Let's cross here," I instructed. "Look, there is a big log on the other side. After you wade across, the log will keep you out of the wind. Ladies, you should go first. Take off your jackets and hold them above the water so you'll have something dry to put on."

Anne led the women across the water, which was up to their hips. Thankfully, they crossed easily without any problems. They found a large log that blocked the cold wind and the sand from stinging their faces.

While the tide rose, the rest of us waited for Ron. I refused to leave my friend behind. He finally arrived an hour later, during high tide. I told Ron we'd found a calm place up the river and planned to swim across the river there.

He disagreed. He wanted to walk on the surf where the river met the ocean. He reminded me that he was a strong swimmer and knew how to handle rip tides and heavy surf. I could not convince him, so Ron set off across the sand while the rest of us walked up the river and prepared to swim. We took off our shoes, tied them together, and hung them around our necks.

Then, we entered the freezing water. The river was broader and colder than we expected, and when we finally reached the other side, we found our radios and phones wet and useless. Our waterproof bags could not fight submersion for such a long time. Now, we had no way to contact our van drivers and were at least an hour past the time they'd planned to meet us. We walked towards the beach, wet and cold, in soaked shoes.

We could see Ron walking in the surf with his jacket held high above his head. He was moving through water up to his chest, but somehow, he made it to the other side of the river. I was relieved to see him safe but worried because he was soaking wet and chilled to the bone. His lips were gray, and his body was shaking.

Unfortunately, we had a three-mile walk to get to the parking lot. We decided to walk as quickly as possible to warm up and then return to anyone who could not keep up, bringing them jackets and dry blankets. Ron was not able to keep up but urged us to go on without him.

In time, we reached the vans waiting for us in the designated spot. We hopped in and started the engines to warm in the heater and dry off. Two of the other men and I gathered dry clothes and a blanket for Ron and returned to the trail to find him.

We walked and walked. There was no sign of Ron anywhere. After searching for more than ninety minutes, we gave up and returned to the vans. There was nothing to do except call 911. We made the call and then drove to our hotel to wait.

When we got to the hotel, it was almost 7 p.m. We were cold, hungry, and worried. As we entered the reception area, we asked the staff if they'd seen Ron. They pointed to a man sitting in a chair fast asleep and covered in blankets. It was Ron.

He explained that he became so cold and tired he could not go on. He saw a residential complex behind the dunes, so he walked there and asked for help. A kind resident gave him blankets and a ride to the hotel. We were all so relieved he was okay, but I felt extremely frustrated with him. Ron was a character who always made us laugh but certainly had a mind of his own. His adventurous spirit was both a joy and a challenge.

As we moved further north along the trail, we encountered vast forests and the majestic redwoods. In some areas, we could see the ocean as we hiked under a canopy of towering trees. Another year, we ended our trip by walking across the Golden Gate Bridge, which was such a thrill we started our walk there the following year so we could cross the bridge again.

Some days, I wanted to pinch myself. It felt like a dream walking in such incredible natural beauty. I fell more in love with the California Coastal Trail every day.

One of the most beautiful sections waited for us at Usal Beach and in the Demonstration Forest. We walked up a narrow dirt road away from the beach up to a plateau in the forest. There was a small, deserted village there, about 300 yards above the black sand beach. Everything was silent and serene as we hiked through wildflowers and verdant greenery.

When we arrived at the Sinkyone Wilderness State Park, we had to leave the trail and travel by van. Recent heavy rains had damaged the trail and some of the bridges. It was too dangerous to hike; even the drive was treacherous. As I drove one of the vans, I recalled driving the bakery van on the wet and slippery dirt roads in Rhodesia's tribal areas.

It took about two hours to travel the twenty miles to the Needle Rock Visitors Center, where it was safe to rejoin the trail and walk towards Orchard Crest Camp.

A terrible thing happened during our 2015 trip. Ron had a stroke on the trail near Shelter Cove. His condition was so severe he had to be airlifted to the city of Redding. Everyone felt shocked because Ron was our court jester and intrepid adventurer. There was nothing to do except hope for the best and walk on.

As we continued north, we reached the Lost Coast. This section of the Lost Coast is so remote the only way to access it is on foot. It is too rugged for highways, and many of the dirt roads wash away during rainy seasons. There is no cell phone coverage on the Lost Coast, so I had to make sure our radios were fully charged and working properly in that area. As we walked, we saw whales jumping from the water, along with otters and seals.

We were all anxious about Ron, but the overwhelming natural beauty before our eyes soothed our spirits.

Ron would never walk the trail with us again. He had additional strokes and eventually lost his eyesight. Ron was the first person to suggest we walk the CCT back in 2000 and walked with us every year until 2015. It seemed unfair he would not complete the journey after all these years, especially since we were on the final stretch.

When we began our annual walk in 2016, Anne's sister Charlotte traveled from England to walk with us. She moved from

Durban to London after the crime there became unbearable. Anne's other sister Helen and her husband Rink traveled from South Africa to walk with us, as well.

As we began our eight-day trek, Pany and his wife Cheryl met us for breakfast in San Rafael before we drove to Eureka, where our journey would begin.

During this section of the CCT, we crossed a vast steel bridge over the Mad River and progressed through lush green vegetation and incredible scenery. We saw lighthouses, walked under giant trees, and near beautiful coves and inlets. Even though we were often up walking on cliffs, we could hear the roar of the waves and catch glimpses of the sea along the twisting trail.

At one point, we walked on an old stagecoach road for about seven miles through dense vegetation and huge trees. It was hard to imagine how pioneers traveled through such challenging terrain.

We traveled through deep forest for the bulk of this trip. Everything was so green.

At Patrick's Point State Park, the trail led us back down to the beach. We stayed along the water until we reached Big Lagoon State Park, the end of that year's walk. We had a beautiful dinner and talked about next year when we would finally arrive at the Oregon border after sixteen years on the CCT.

I could just imagine walking across that border, proud of the countless hours I'd invested planning and overseeing the group for so many years. I was already planning a grand celebration to mark the end of this momentous physical and logistical challenge, one of the biggest goals I'd ever set for myself.

It seemed like nothing would stop me or slow me down. It was exhilarating and exciting to know the next CCT walk would be our last.

Chapter 27: The End of the Trail

➤

After we completed our 2016 CCT walk, Anne took a long time to recover. Later that year, Charlotte organized a wonderful family reunion in Scotland, renting a castle for the extended family and then a five-day cruise on a river barge along the Union Canal to Edinburgh. It was a wonderful experience, but Anne was plagued by knee pain and a profound tiredness.

Finally, Anne was diagnosed with plural mesothelioma, a grueling form of cancer in the lung lining caused from exposure to asbestos. My beautiful wife, who never smoked and always took good care of her health, was stricken with a devastating illness and a poor prognosis. Mesothelioma is a terrible illness, stealing breath, life, and vitality quickly from those caught in its clutches. No cure exists. She was exposed to asbestos when her family lived by an asbestos mine that her father managed.

Nikki immediately moved home from Texas to help, and she and Athena cared for Anne tenderly through every step of her illness. Pany flew in every other weekend from San Francisco. Anne's sisters and many other friends visited, as well. The outpouring of support we received gave us strength during some very dark days.

There are no words to describe my profound pain seeing my wonderful wife suffer. I canceled the CCT walk in May of 2017 because I would not leave Anne for any reason. I was not sure I wanted to finish the trail without Anne by my side.

I spent hours holding her hand and talking about our beautiful life together. I felt so helpless watching her suffer.

As she was deteriorating, Anne made me promise to do two things: complete the final leg of the CCT and write a book about my life story. I had to keep those final promises to her, no matter how painful.

Life seemed so unfair. Anne saw fourteen different doctors and associates, along with as many supportive therapies as we could try. Despite our every effort and many different treatments, my beloved Anne passed away in June of 2017, just ten months after her diagnosis.

Our family was devastated and mourned deeply together. I am eternally grateful for Nikki, Pany, and Athena, who gave me all their love and support during this horrible time. Truthfully, losing Anne was the most challenging experience of my life. It was worse than being forced to go to war. I felt like I'd lost half of my body, heart, and soul.

It was almost impossible for me to stay in our house where I encountered memories of Anne in every room. Linda, our good friend and realtor, helped me sell it and find a smaller home.

It took some time, but I was able to plan the remaining CCT walk. I promised Anne I'd finish it, even though it was terrible to think of walking the trail without her. I felt no joy while planning— none of my typical excitement, just profound sorrow. I wasn't sure how I would be able to endure this walk, but I felt Anne would be with me every step of the way just as I'd felt with Gerry in Kefalonia.

On Saturday, May 12, 2018, my group of walkers and I flew to Oakland to begin the final leg of our 1,200-mile odyssey. After seventeen years, I looked forward to completing the goal I'd set for us so long ago. Due to busy schedules and other commitments, no one in our walking group had been able to walk every step of the trail except for me. I missed Anne and Ron dreadfully.

While I was planning the trip, I contacted Richard Nichols and Bob Lorentzen, authors of the guidebooks that enabled me to design the trips so successfully. Richard and Bob agreed to walk part of the trail with our group.

I also notified Cea Higgins, the California Coastal Trail's Executive Director. Cea also arranged for some county supervisors from Del Norte county, and a local reporter to walk with us and cover the story. She planned to join us for the last day too.

Finishing this walk was a huge accomplishment, and many people wanted to celebrate it with us.

Before our walk, torrential rains buffeted that area of California. In my preparatory calls with park rangers, I learned some areas of the trail were impassable. We'd also have to be very careful because it was mating season for elks. An elk can be more dangerous than a bear during mating season, so we had to be extremely cautious on the trail. Even during the final miles of this long journey, I had to plan carefully and be very aware of safety issues.

After flying to Oakland and traveling by van, we began our walk on Sunday morning at Big Lagoon State Park, walking on the sandy beach there. The day was overcast, windy, and cool, but our spirits were high. Soon we entered the majestic Redwood Forest and enjoyed touring the visitor center there.

On Monday morning, a group of fifteen hikers coming north on that trail from Eureka joined our walk for the day. They'd heard of our journey and wanted to hike with us for a few hours to give us their support. They were delightful people and gave me tips about navigating that section of the CCT.

Over the following days, we walked through some of the most incredible scenery on earth. The giant redwood trees, beaches, big wide rivers, and forest pathways were breathtaking. Because of all the rain, everything was very green. In some places, grass grew higher than my knees and covered the trail.

As I walked in this incredible beauty, I missed Anne dreadfully but knew she was looking down on me and encouraging me as she'd always done. I had time to think about my long life and marvel that a little boy from Patras, Greece was lucky enough to travel to so many places and have so many adventures. The surrounding beauty began to heal my broken heart.

On Thursday, author Richard Nichols and his wife Brenda met us at the Crescent City Lighthouse. They would walk with us until the end of the trail. I felt thrilled to meet Richard and thank him for making the journey possible. His guidebooks made the trip planning so much easier.

We walked near Lake Talawa and Lake Earl that day. Millions of mosquitos swarmed around us, so thick we all walked close together so we could try to move them off each other. Even bug spray did not deter them.

After our walk ended that day, I had a particular task to perform. One of my walkers, Joe, is a licensed surveyor from San Diego. He and I got some GPS equipment from a friend and went out to find the precise spot where the CCT crosses the border into Oregon. There is some dispute about the exact location.

After we located the spot, we put down markers, so we'd know exactly when we crossed the line based on the GPS coordinate. We also walked in the adjacent woods and marked a place there as well. Then, Joe and I drove to the Crescent City airport to pick up Pany and Athena who would walk the final two days of the trail with me. I was overjoyed to share the end of the CCT with them.

On Friday, we walked on Kellogg beach, through the forest to Yontocket, then up to the Smith River. That evening we had a grand dinner celebration with all the walkers, Richard and Brenda, and Pany and Athena. Bob Lorentzen, the other author of the guidebooks, and Cea Higgins drove up seven hours from the Bay Area with friends and family members to join us for dinner and walk the final leg of the CCT with us the following morning. We shared stories of our adventures along the trail, as well as our appreciation for the remarkable opportunity to experience the California coast.

Yet, I scarcely slept that night. While I felt proud and happy I'd reached my goal after so many years, I was also sad to reach the end of a journey that gave me such joy for so many years without Anne by my side. I could scarcely believe it was ending at last.

As I tossed and turned that night, my life passed before my eyes. I thought of my parents and Anne. They'd been part of every significant moment of my life, so I hoped they were watching me now.

We met at 8:30 that morning at the mouth of the Smith River at the Ship Shore Resort with the county supervisors, their families, and even some of their pet dogs. The Del Norte dignitaries gave a short presentation. Then the reporter conducted interviews. At 9 a.m. sharp, we all began walking the final five miles of the California Coastal Trail along the beach. We passed the massive rock at Pyramid Point to the sound of thundering waves.

"Here we are, Pelican Beach at last!" I said when we were near the end of our journey. "Let's all form a long line across the beach. Everyone hold hands. We are going to cross this line together!"

I took Pany and Athena's hands as the rest of the group joined the long line. "Ready, set, go!" I shouted.

Together we crossed the border line Joe and I marked the previous day, then we continued onward another two hundred feet to the other spot some call the end of the CCT, ensuring we covered every step of the trail. We'd reached Oregon!

After we finished the walk and exchanged hugs and handshakes, we placed a plaque in the forest on the second spot Joe and I marked, commemorating our journey and in loving memory of Anne. As we placed the plaque, I thought of the day Ron, Gary, Phil, and I first discussed walking the CCT back in 2000. Eighteen years later, I stood at the end of the trail with a full heart and tears in my eyes.

We celebrated with a grand party. Before the trip, I created a playlist of special music. Pany and Athena had arranged for pizzas, champagne, and juice. It was a grand celebration. I even drank a small bit of champagne to mark the occasion, one of the few times in my life I consumed alcohol. As we gathered on the sand, we ate pizza, toasted our success, and rejoiced over our accomplishment.

Then, we danced.

From top left (clockwise): My brother and me in Greece: Chapter 1; With my friend in front of the bakery van that carried Robert Mugabe: Chapter 6; My pet monkey, Sally: Chapter 4; The first van I drove when I was 14: Chapter 5.

From top left (clockwise): Anne and me in front of the bridge connecting Rhodesia and Zambia on the Zambezi River: Chapter 8; Anne and I with our pet, Pixie: Chapter 8; Anne and me in Gatooma in our 20's: Chapter 8.

From top to bottom: On our honeymoon visiting the Parthenon on the Acropolis: Chapter 8; With my car Vauxhall Cresta in Gatooma: Chapter 8.

From top to bottom: The main building of the Coronet drive-in: Chapter 9; My family at my daughter Nikki's christening from left to right: my sister-in-law Angela, my mother, my sweet Anne, me, my father, my sister Cathreen, my brother Peter: Chapter 13.

From top left (clockwise): Holding my oldest daughter Nikki at Cape Agulhas, the most southern point of the African continent: Chapter 15; Holding my three beloved treasures: Chapter 19; Holding my son Pany in a game park amongst ostriches: Chapter 15.

From top to bottom: One of the teams I coached won the championship: Chapter 16 and 17; My family and home in Durban: Chapter 14.

From top to bottom: The load runner with some of my distributors: Chapter 18;
Me and my brother with our children and a friend on one of my flying visits:
Chapter 15 and 16; My daughter Nikki, sister-in-law Angela, brother, me, his son
George in front of part of Springhawk complex.: Chapter 18.

From top to bottom: La Jolla House: Chapter 21; Steele's stepmother, Pany, Anne, Lionel, Steele, me, and my sister: Chapter 22.

From top to bottom: My family and my brother's family on a road trip: Chapter 24; Taking a break in Bodega Bay during our CCT walk: Chapter 26 and 27.

From top to bottom: My San Diego soccer group photo. I am 3rd in the middle from the right, wearing a ball cap: Chapter 16 and 17; Before the morning walk in Kefalonia: Chapter 25; At the Resort at Smith's River before starting our final day of the walk. Athena is in the middle, me and Pany are to the right: Chapter 27.

From top left (clockwise): CCT California to Oregon crossing: Chapter 27; Family picture: Pany, Nikki, Anne, Athena, and me: Chapter 22.; Me and my walkers in the entrance to the Golden Gate Bridge walking CCT North: Chapter 26.

From top to bottom: Leading the Zorba dancing in Kefalonia: Chapter 25; Anne and I at Lake Tahoe: Chapter 24.

Appendix: Living Your Life with No Limits

It gives me immense joy to mentor people, sharing the lessons I've learned over the course of more than fifty years as a business owner. These success pillars support a life of success and satisfaction with no limits, regardless of what type of work you pursue.

1. Don't fear failure. If things don't work as you'd envisioned, learn from that experience, make changes, improve things, and move on to your next success. As seen in chapter 4.
2. Always seek knowledge. You have nothing to lose and much to gain. As read in chapter 5.
3. Cultivate a positive reputation. Found in chapters 6 and 18.
4. Trust in yourself and be confident in your decisions. Read in chapters 7, 17, and 18.
5. Focus on providing the best quality products and best customer service. Found in chapter 9.
6. Seek guides and mentors. Portrayed in chapter 13.

7. Assemble the right team and train them well to succeed and win. As seen in chapters 14, 15, and 17.

8. Communicate with respect and solicit feedback so you can constantly improve. As read in chapter 15.

9. Every business can be improved. Make continuous improvement to your goal. Found in chapter 17.

10. Beautify your environment to increase productivity and satisfaction. Portrayed in chapter 18.

11. Be nimble and ready to adapt quickly to changing conditions. Read in chapter 19.

12. Create a compelling vision of your success and let it give you energy and the desire to succeed. As found in chapters 14 and 21.

13. Always have a well-considered plan before you begin a project. Executed throughout my life, but especially in chapter 23.

14. Invest your time and energy on projects for which you feel passion. As read in chapter 24.

15. Celebrate as often as possible. Every success is an opportunity to celebrate with your family, friends, and employees. As portrayed in chapters 18, 25, 26, and 27.

Acknowledgements

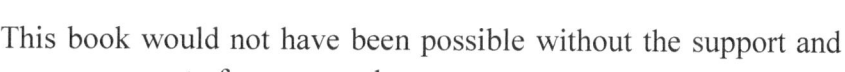

This book would not have been possible without the support and encouragement of many people.

First, I must honor and thank my remarkable children, my beloved treasures.

My daughter, Nikki, a gifted writer and published author. Nikki has guided me through the entire process of creating this book from the very beginning to its completion. She gave generously of her time, ideas, and creative thinking.

My daughter Athena supported me with advice and encouragement. Her meticulous care and organization of thousands of family photographs enabled me to refresh my memory and find the perfect photos for this book.

My son Pany always gives me wise counsel and support. He encouraged me to keep writing and reminded me of some important details.

I must also thank my friend Gary for his ideas and suggestions, especially on the sections about the California Coastal Trail and Kefalonia walks.

I send my thanks to my family and friends in Greece, Southern Africa, Australia, Canada, and the United States for all their wonderful contributions. Every story in this book happened because of the people who loved and supported me during all my adventures.

To Cea Higgins and everyone involved in the California Coastal Trail Association, thank you for creating one of the most remarkable walking trails in the world. I enjoyed walking every step. Bob Lorentzen and Richard Nichols, your CCT trail guides kept me and my group safe and comfortable for 1,200 miles. I thank you for all your thorough research and for joining us as we completed the final leg of our journey.

I also thank those professionals who worked tirelessly to shape my story into the book you hold in your hands today. Additional writing by Lynne Klippel transformed my story over many months of long conversations, rough drafts, and brainstorming together. Michelle Vandepas and her team made the process of publishing and marketing the book an exciting and enjoyable experience.

Finally, I would like to thank each of you who are reading this book. I hope it inspires you to make your life exactly the way you wish it to be.

About the Author

Nick Haritatos is a successful entrepreneur, soccer player, pilot, and devoted family man whose career spanned four countries on three continents. From his humble beginnings in war-torn Greece to southern Africa, Haritatos began a remarkable journey to success, buying his first business at sixteen and creating a portfolio of successful companies in Rhodesia, South Africa, and the United States.

Buffeted by winds of sweeping change, Nick pledged to make his own destiny, regardless of any obstacles. He lived a life of adventure set amidst mud huts and dirt roads in tribal lands in Africa, harrowing days of the Rhodesian Bush War, numerous board rooms, international trips to over forty countries, and one-of-a-kind ocean view homes.

His business career stretches across twenty-three companies and over fifty years in manufacturing, retail, service, and commercial, retail, and residential real estate. With a knack for spotting untapped potential in businesses and people, Nick treasures his vast network of friends as intensely as his financial success. He loves to celebrate life with music and dancing whenever possible.

Early on, Nick developed a unique and flexible lifestyle model that allowed him to oversee multiple businesses simultaneously while devoting plenty of time to his wife and children. With his decision to create his own destiny, Nick maintains control over his life and his future even under challenging circumstances, when most others followed tradition. His motto is "I make events. Events don't make me."

An avid athlete, Nick has played and coached soccer for most of his life. Nick has team members who've played soccer with him for nearly twenty-five years in San Diego. As of the writing of this book, he's played in more than 2,500 matches, as well as completed several marathons. He plans to be playing soccer when he is eighty years old and beyond.

Outside of his family and business success, one of his proudest achievements was hiking the 1,200-mile California Coastal Trail.

Today Nick uses his considerable business and life experience to mentor and inspire a new generation of entrepreneurs and business leaders when he isn't on the soccer field or planning his next walk.

Nick is available to speak to groups interested in business and personal success. For more information on his speaking and mentoring work, visit his website at www.nolimitsbynick.com

www.ingramcontent.com/pod-product-compliance
Lightning Source LLC
Chambersburg PA
CBHW060910120626
46553CB00001B/278